SINSEMILLA *to* SINS FORGIVEN

From Mind Blowing Marijuana to Jesus

JOHNNY ZAPATA

Scripture quotations marked KJV are from the King James Version of the Bible. Scripture quotations marked NKJV are from the New King James Version of the Bible.

ISBN: 979-8-89031-673-8 (sc)
ISBN: 979-8-89031-674-5 (hc)
ISBN: 979-8-89031-675-2 (e)

One Galleria Blvd., Suite 1900, Metairie, LA 70001
(504) 702-6708

CONTENTS

ACKNOWLEDGMENTS

I am very thankful to God Almighty for giving me the parents He did; they taught me to never give up in life. I am also thankful to God for a true friend He allowed me to make at the RIT, who gave me my first laptop to help me, start dictating *Sinsemilla to Sins Forgiven.* I am very appreciative to my whole family, along with my personal assistant, for helping me numerous times to get set up on my computer. When I was working on this manuscript and had to stay in bed, my wife reminded me not to be turned on any certain side too long or, if I was up in the wheelchair, not to stay sitting so long, in order to prevent pressure sores. I thank her for always looking out for me.

INTRODUCTION

I was blessed to start working at the Kewanee Nursery when I was fifteen years old, and I hadn't even started messing around with witchcraft yet. A little after my sixteenth birthday, I was married to a beautiful, young Latina woman, and about the same time, I became the owner of a few books, all dealing with the occult. Since I was dabbling with witchcraft at that time, I believed that was the reason for me being in the right place at the right time. I also believed that was the reason things were going nice and smooth for me. But the truth was I had the favor of God Almighty on me.

At a faster than regular pace, I was promoted to the position of foreman of a digging crew. I hadn't even been on a digging crew before and had absolutely no experience digging. After an encounter with my cousin, Arthur, I was able to meet and become friends with people who did and dealt street drugs, especially marijuana.

My life seemed to be flying on autopilot; just when I thought things couldn't get any better, I would get another big-time blessing. I was able to see and do a lot of things that I know I would not have had the chance to experience if I had lived a normal life. From the young age of sixteen, to the slightly more mature age of twenty-four, it felt like I was living my life in hyper speed. I was the boss of a digging crew at the nursery where I worked, and I was the boss at what I like to call my second job.

I didn't ever think I would reach the age of sixty-two, much less that I'd be in a wheelchair for over thirty-eight years. I will always remember 1985; from start to finish, it was a very memorable year for me. To start out with, before I turned twenty-four that year, I experienced, for the first time ever in my life, a big betrayal. It felt like I had been stabbed in the back and then the knife had been twisted around and around inside of me. If I would have given the person who betrayed me a reason to do so, then I would have felt like maybe I deserved it. I always tried to treat people the way I wanted to be treated, and that was fairly and with respect.

The year had not started out looking so good for me, but as far as I was concerned, I had life by the tail. Even though I was messing around with the underground, in a manner of speaking, just about every single night, I still remembered to pray to God Almighty.

I thank God Almighty for His Word. He says in Romans, "And we know that all things work together for good to those that love God, to those who are the called according to His purpose" (Romans 8:28 NKJV).

At the time of the accident, I initially couldn't see how everything was going to work out for the good, but after a few years had passed by, I was able to see. This is why I wrote *Sinsemilla to Sins Forgiven*. I hope, pray, and believe that whoever reads it will learn what I learned without having to go through what I went through.

CHAPTER 1

IN THE BEGINNING GOD

You would never have imagined just by looking at the little three-year-old ball of fire that, when he grew to the young age of sixteen, he would literally start his journey through the valley of the shadow of death, but with no fear as in Psalms 23:4. The year was 1964. His mom and dad were both in their early twenties and from a small border town in South Texas by the name of Las Palomas in Starr County. If you went to the outskirts of town and—since the Texas riverbank side was so much higher than the Mexican riverbank side—if you had a good strong arm, you could literally throw a rock from the United States to Mexico. The father of the little boy—who had been born on July 24, 1961 and given the name Johnny Zapata—would take him to that river often. I was that little boy.

At that time, I was the older of two children, and our parents were migrant workers. In winter or early spring, depending on how the weather was behaving, they would travel to different places they knew of for work. Or if they heard from other people that some work hands were needed somewhere, they would go quickly and find out if they could get the job. You know how that old saying goes, "The early bird gets the worm." That way, they could make some money in order for us to live more comfortably.

My parents' work would usually be some kind of manual labor—out in a field dealing with some kind of fruits or vegetables, baling hay or stacking it, picking cotton or asparagus. They took whatever kind of work they could get and they were both willing and able to get it done. And they always did their very best. They were taught to be light on their feet; that teaching came from my grandparents on my dad's side. Our houses were right next to each other. My mom had been taught to work as long as she was able to stand up. What I mean by that is, even if she was in her eighth or ninth month of pregnancy, she was working out in the fields doing something. Keep in mind, she had a total of nine children. She was a strong woman.

My mother's name was Anna, and my dad's name was Beto Jr. When they went to work, whichever one of us Zapata children had been born most recently would get to stay with either my mom or my Grandma Zapata. They would take turns staying at home and watching us. Depending on where they were working, if other families had children who needed to be taken care of, either my mom or grandma would be willing to watch them also. At first, there wasn't very many of us Zapata children, but as the years went by, we began to grow in numbers. If my mom just had a baby who needed to be nursed, then, of course, she would be the one staying at home.

Since my Grandma and Grandpa Zapata would travel with us, they would also be ready to work at the drop of a hat. Because of them, my mom and dad learned to be hard workers; also a lot of our ways of thinking came from them. One lesson my grandparents stuck to firmly, which we too believed, went like this: "If you think you're man enough to stay out drinking until the next morning, you better be man enough to get up in the morning for work," My dad, in turn, passed those words and beliefs on to his children, and since I was the firstborn, I heard and saw those words in action the longest.

In our hometown of Las Palomas, just about everybody was related in one way or another. For the most part, everybody got along with each other. But there were times when somebody drank too much or did some kind of drugs. Then it was the alcohol or the drugs that were in control of them, instead of them being in control of the alcohol or the drugs, so that meant they were out of control. That's when the stuff would hit the fan, and the negative situations would start manifesting, even between the best of friends or relatives.

One day, my aunt Norma came over to visit at our house. When she got there, I was playing with some of my action figures on the floor. I overheard her telling my mom about an incident that her son, Sammy, had witnessed from the playground. Apparently, during recess, two men had been cleaning a piece of land across the street from the school. The men were working with machetes. "A friend of his who was at the far end of the playground started pointing and shouting, 'Fight! Fight!'" my aunt said. She went on to report that the two men went at each other with the machetes and did nasty damage to each other. "Thank God it lasted only for a brief moment."

"What happened?" my mom wanted to know.

My aunt leaned over toward my mom and said, "When everything was finally over, one of the men had a gash on the left side of his face and was trying to get up off the ground. The other one had quickly started walking away. He was bleeding very badly from the top of his left arm. The poor children who were outside for recess got to see graphic violence in action; it was terrible."

"My goodness," my mom gasped.

After telling her story, my aunt said she had to get home to start supper. "I will see you all later, God willing." She waved as she left.

My mom said, "Okay, you make sure to say hi to the family."

Later it was known that both men were brothers and had been drinking since early in the morning. That didn't help the situation out. All of that because of some alcohol and a small piece of land.

My dad would always repeat the words he heard my grandpa saying, and this was one of his favorite sayings: "Whatever it is that you're doing, always do the best you can. Be light on your feet, and people will take notice of you and the work you do." Since my dad both heard and did that everywhere he went, eventually, the right people did take notice. And that's why he ended up being the number one boss man at a tree and shrub nursery.

After a year had gone by, my parents and grandparents thought I was old enough, so they would let me help out; that way, I could learn by experience. One day, my grandpa saw that his house needed to be reshingled; he chose wood shingles because he thought they would last longer than the other types of roofing shingles that were available at the time and he liked the way they looked. My dad and grandpa decided to do the job themselves. Besides, at the moment, they had no extra money to pay someone else to do the job. They had a ladder leaning against the side of the house where they were bringing the bundles of shingles up, but curiosity got the best of me, and that wouldn't be the last time either. I saw them going up and down the ladder, so when they were busy on the roof and nobody on the ground was paying attention, I decided to climb up the ladder and see for myself what all the hammering noise was about.

When they saw me, they were surprised. My dad said, "Hey, what are you doing up here?"

I said, "I just wanted to see what was happening because I heard a bunch of noise up here."

They hadn't heard me when I was climbing up because I was being extra quiet and really careful, so I wouldn't miss a step while I was on my way up.

They told me to go back down slowly, and that was my first of many daring adventures. They kept an extra eye on me from that time on and told me not to climb up the ladder unless a grown person was watching me. They started noticing from that day on that I wasn't very easily intimidated.

It didn't take the two men that long, and soon, they'd reshingled the entire roof.

This was during wintertime, but where we lived, wintertime wasn't that cold. Once the sun came up, the day would get warm. But sometimes, on certain nights, it would be downright cold. My mom and grandma would get some wood together and make a fire. That would keep us warm if we were outside and because we didn't have a heater in either one of our houses. After the fire had been going for a while, the wood would get burned up really well, so no more smoke would be coming out of the burned wood, but it would have turned into red-hot embers. Usually it would be my dad who would get the two biggest washtubs we had and then fill them up about a quarter of the way with dirt. Afterward, he'd scoop up some embers from the bottom of the fire and put them on top of the dirt in the washtubs. Then my mom and grandma together would put the tubs in the middle of the room where we were going to be sleeping. They would place each tub on top of four bricks spaced evenly apart on the floor in the shape of a circle. The bricks created extra space between the hot embers and the wooden floors. The tubs were set in the middle of the rooms so the heat would be distributed evenly all around that area. We would make sure furniture and other things that could catch on fire were not too close to our heaters.

When my mom and grandma first brought the tubs in, we would be able to stand close to them and warm ourselves up for a couple of minutes, but then we would have to get away. They weren't the most modern heaters at that time, but they did work for us.

Our homes were humble but clean. My mom and dad's house consisted of just one big, open room. We didn't have any walls dividing the kitchen area where we would eat from the area where we would sleep and watch TV. On the other hand, my grandparent's house was a little bigger; they had a kitchen and a living room/bedroom area, which were divided by a wall. When you came in the front door, you would walk into the kitchen. There was a wall and a doorway to the right, but if you walked in through the doorway, you would be in the living room/ bedroom area. In the middle of that space was where we would put our washtub heater. I always thought my grandparent's house was bigger and just so cool!

I really didn't know any better. The year was 1965, and we didn't really get out that much. The relatives that we did go visit sometimes had houses that were built a little different, but all of them had their kitchen, living room, and bedroom areas. We didn't ever envy what other people had; we weren't raised that way. Our parents and grandparents would always say, "If somebody else has nicer things than you, be glad for them. It is good that God has blessed them like that." For instance, my grandparent's on my mother's side, the Lusianos, were a lot better off when it came down to money than my grandparents on my dad's side, the Zapatas.

I always thought of my grandpas as being the last real, live cowboys in the world; the best part of it all was they were my grandpas. My Grandpa Luciano always had horses and cows to take care of. His two sons and, if necessary, hired hands at times, would help him out. We would go and visit them sometimes, and their house was bigger than what I was used to seeing. Close to the end of that year, my grandpa had a new brick home built for his family. When you walked in the front door, you would be in the living room. If you kept on going straight and through a doorway, you would be in the kitchen with a small dining area; that's also where the back door was. When you were back in the living room, instead of going straight into the kitchen, if you turned to the left and went down a hallway, you could either go to a sitting room with a nice-sized console TV and a brown vinyl couch that could be turned into a bed or, if you kept on going, you could pick from one of three bedrooms. They each had their own little electric heaters in case we had a cold front come down from the north. But I didn't ever once think or say that I would rather live at their house or that we should have what they had at our house. I thought it was great God had blessed them like that, and I felt blessed to have both sides when it came to grandparents. As far as I was concerned, I had the best grandparents in the world.

Another thing I felt good about was that we always had fresh fruit in the house; if we didn't buy fruit when we went grocery shopping, we'd see a man by the name of Nacho who lived in town. He would go and buy bushel baskets and sacks full of Ruby Red grapefruits, oranges, and tangerines. Then he would drive his truck all around town, honking his horn to see who wanted to buy fruit from him at a nice, low price. That would be another big-time blessing and a half because, if the people who had gone grocery shopping had forgotten to get fruit, they could always flag down Nacho the fruit man, as he was known. They could choose from what he had inside the cab or the back of his truck. He would make it available to whoever needed fruit, and as that old saying goes,

"That was better than a jab in the eye with a sharp stick any day." We always had fresh fruit, and most of the time, it was thanks to Nacho.

I remember the first time I ever tried a cooked orange. That was one of the times that my grandma had asked me, "Will you help me gather up some wood so I can start a fire?"

"Sure, Grandma," I said. I would be right there whenever she was going to do anything, especially if she was going to make a fire.

Later on that evening, after my dad had gotten home, he was warming himself by the fire. He went in the house and got five nice big oranges. The fire had been burning for a while, so the flames had gone down quite a bit. He put three of the oranges around the outer edge of the fire. That way, they could get warmed up on one side. Then he turned them on their other side for a few more minutes. He took one of them out and replaced it with one of the two that were left. He carefully peeled the one he took out and asked me, "Do you want to try some of my orange?"

"Sure, Dad." After I tried it, that was it. From then on, I found one more thing in life that I really liked—cooked oranges. Well, they really weren't cooked, but I called them cooked. The outside of the orange would get a little burnt-looking, but after my dad got the peel off, the inside was nice and warm. It would also have a little mesquite flavor to boot; we always used mesquite wood to make the fires because mesquite trees grew freely all over in that part of Texas.

One day, I was in my grandmother's kitchen, and I had an orange in my hand. My grandma knew that I couldn't peel oranges by myself and I needed someone to start it off for me. She asked me, "What are you going to do with that orange?"

"I'm going to eat it," I told her.

She said, "You can't do that; you can't peel it yourself."

Without missing a beat or saying anything to anybody, I just grabbed the orange in my right hand, nice and tight, and, *BAM!* I threw it on the kitchen floor, as if I were a major league pitcher. When the orange hit the floor, it split a little, but that was all I needed to peel it myself. That was one of many confidence builders for me.

The next day, some of my dad's friends came by and invited him to go hunting. They left around eight o'clock in the morning, and after a few hours, about twelve o'clock, they returned, just in time for lunch. They brought with them a bunch of mourning doves. They knew what fields the doves would gather at, so that's where they went hunting for the birds with various-sized shotguns. My mom and grandma helped out by starting a fire. They also helped clean the birds and season them up. Meanwhile, the perfect amount of time had passed by so that the fire was just right for cooking. They would spread out the embers and have me go find four empty tin cans. Then they would put them on the four corners where the evenly spread out embers were ready for the grill. The grill we had was constructed from an old refrigerator, which we would use whenever cooking anything outside over an open fire. At the time, we had plenty of meat—*dove meat* but nevertheless meat. That was a big-time blessing.

Five days later, at the perfect time, when we were almost running out of meat, my dad's friends came by the house once again. They were all talking about going fishing. They put an old fishing net they'd been given, which was stored at our place, in the back of my dad's truck. They'd already fixed up the net, adding long boards along both ends, so that two people could easily hold the net open and drag it in the water. Our small town was right next to the Rio Grande River, and every once in a while, the river would overflow its banks and some fields in low areas would get flooded. That would be a blessing and a half for my dad and his friends, all of us really. After the water would start drying up, what would be left over in those low spots would be fish, lots of fish, and some of them were nice and big. The men would go down to the low spots, and two of them would hold their net open wide on one side of the flooded field. The rest of them would get into the water a little distance away and start making noise while walking toward the net. Whatever fish were in front of them would start heading toward the net. The young man farthest away would bring his end toward the shore, and success. That was the plan for this particular day—to check out some of those flooded fields.

After driving around for a little while, my dad and his friends saw that something was making a big wave in one certain spot. It was a little distance from them, but it got them all excited. They all looked at each other and said, "It's time to go fishing." All of them started pointing and yelling, "Look over there!"

Immediately, Fidel, who was in the back of my dad's truck, grabbed a pitchfork so when they got to the spot where that something was making the big wave, he would be ready for it. They started out like usual. El Gallito and Chano were the net guys, so from the back of the truck, they unloaded the net and began to unroll it. Then they brought it into the water with them. The other guys slowly got in the water on the opposite side, about twenty-five yards away, and started making noise. Soon the men saw what was making the wave, and they all agreed that it was the biggest fish any of them had ever seen. So they started yelling at Fidel, "Stick it! Stick it!"

With his heart pumping and his adrenaline rushing, Fidel grabbed the pitchfork tight in his hands and drove it deep into the fish's back. As the fish took off with the pitchfork stuck in its back, it looked like a submarine with its periscope out of the water. One of the young men, Angelo, ran to the truck and got a .22 rifle my dad always had with him. He started shooting at the fish where he thought its head should be. After five shots, the fish stopped moving.

All the men were excited to see what that big fish looked like out on dry land. Since El Gallito had the side of the net that was farthest out, he brought his side, in and with it came a bunch of good, regular-size fish. They each were at least sixteen inches long, nice and meaty. Plus that wave maker was a great big garfish that was over six feet long from nose to tail. It was nice and round and full of meat.

The men put all the good, regular-size fish, along with the monster garfish, on an old tarp my dad always carried with him so they could easily load up their catch in the back of the truck and went home. Did they ever have a fish story to tell. Everybody was happy!

After my dad and his friends drove home, they put all the smaller fish in a big washtub, cleaned them up, and divided the big catch among themselves. Everybody got plenty of the regular-size fish. And after that big gar got cleaned and cut into pieces, they all got a big piece of him too.

Everyone had his own version of the way things happened that day. When it came to the regular-size fish, now that was one thing. But when it came to the six foot-long monster gar, they didn't just have the story. What was even better was they also had the meat to go with it. I thank God, the Creator of the heavens and the earth, the Alpha and Omega, the Beginning and the End, the First and the Last; my family and I didn't ever want for anything.

Although we lived a pretty simple life, at the same time, we always had everything we needed to live. We thought everything was normal and the way it should be. We ate a lot of pinto beans, rice with meat, or spaghetti with meat, Mexican-style of course, with just the right spices and a lot of love added to it, which always made everything taste better.

Because we had electricity at our houses, we were able to have a couple of refrigerators. They weren't very big, but they served their purpose. We knew of other people who had big box freezers or the stand-up kind. They could either buy a lot of meat, or if they were blessed to own their own animals, some would fatten them up and butcher them, so they could fill their freezers. Since my Grandpa Luciano usually had horses and cows, sometimes he would have a cow butchered. Grandpa Luciano's family was among the families who were blessed to have a big box freezer, so when he'd butcher a cow, his freezer would be nice and full. Whenever that happened, he would always offer us some meat. The way I once heard it put was, "If you want to have friends, you have to first of all show yourself to be friendly," and my grandpa was a pretty friendly man. Everybody in our small town knew him, so whenever one of his friends would kill a deer or a wild boar or anything, they would give him a piece of the meat because he would always do the same.

In addition, there were other times when he and his sons would go take care of his livestock and he would kill an armadillo or a jackrabbit. Usually, whenever he went to check on his livestock, he had a rifle with him, just in case he ran into a rattlesnake. As far as I knew, he never cooked one, but if he would ever decide to, I wouldn't mind trying it.

I heard rattlesnake meat tastes just like chicken, and I like chicken, especially if my grandpa cooked it.

I remember one time we went over to his house, and my grandparents had just made tamales from a combination of wild boar and deer meat. I liked the way they tasted. We later found out the reason for that mixture was wild boar meat was greasy like a pig and the deer meat was kind of dry, but the right mixture was perfect for tamales. My Grandpa Luciano was a good cook; he could toss just about anything together, add the right spices, and he would have a meal.

One morning, my dad took us over to Grandpa Luciano's house. He asked us if we had already eaten breakfast. We all said no, and he told us to sit down. He cooked about six eggs together, added a can of corn, some tomato sauce, and a little salt and pepper, and breakfast was ready.

I remember a special Wednesday morning; my Grandpa Luciano and his two younger sons drove his truck over to my mom and dad's house. He asked, "Can Johnny come with us? We are going to a friend of mines ranch. He has some horses that need to be broken, and we are going to help him. Johnny will be fine. I will take care of him."

I hadn't ever seen anything like that happen in real life, only in Westerns. I thought, *That sounds cool, and I know I'm going to have fun, just like I do every time I go with my grandpa.*

When we finally got to his friend's ranch, my grandpa's youngest son, Mario, had to get out of the truck and open the gate door so we could drive through. Mario jumped in the back of the truck for the rest of the way until we got to the house. After my grandpa introduced me to his friend and everybody said hi, we were off to the corral. I had seen the corral from a distance as we drove close to the house, and I thought it looked quite a bit higher than the normal corrals I had seen before. I looked between the boards, after my grandpa had told his two sons, "Mario and Luis, go where the horses are all together and separate one from the herd. Bring it to this big part of the corral where we are all at." When I saw the size of the first horse that got brought in there, I knew exactly why the corral was so big.

They did exactly that, and with a rope Luis had that looked kind of stiff, he lassoed the horse. I found out later that day the rope that was used is called a *reata* in Spanish. At first I thought it had a wire in the middle, but then I found out it was the material it was made from and how it was made that kept it looking like that.

With the reata around the horse's neck, I helped the men chase the horse around and around in the corral so it would get tired. Luis pulled the rope tighter and tighter until the horse couldn't get any air; all of a sudden, *BAM!* It fell to the ground. Since Luis had the other end of the reata in his hands, he kept tension on the rope while the other men quickly put a cloth bag over the horse's head. Then he loosened the rope, and the animal slowly got up. The men then threw a saddle on its back and fastened it nice and tight. They slowly took the bag off, slipped a bridle in the horse's mouth, and took the rope off its neck while still hanging onto it. Mario got on, and everybody else quickly got away. The horse bucked wildly, trying to get Mario off its back. After the horse got tired and quit bucking, Mario rode it around the corral a few times, and then everything that had been put on the horse was taken off. They brought another one in the big corral area, and the entire process was repeated a few more times.

A little later in the afternoon, Grandpa said, "Let's take a break and go eat lunch."

Valentin, his friend, said, "I've got some meat in the refrigerator, and there's onions, tomatoes, garlic, or whatever else you need in the kitchen."

My grandpa cut up everything real nice and small and then put it in a cast-iron frying pan just at the right time, and he had done it again; lunch tasted real good.

I got to see something that day I had never seen before, and I had a lot of fun helping. I felt super great that day, like God always wanted me to smile and be happy. I had no way of knowing all of the crazy, wild, sometimes dangerous times that were coming my way in the near future. What I did know for sure was that God was always with me because my grandma had told me so.

CHAPTER 2

TRAIN UP A CHILD IN THE WAY HE SHOULD GO

Let me try to paint a clear picture of how it was in late 1965 if you didn't have the luxuries of indoor plumbing. First of all, if the two water barrels that were at the side of my grandparent's house, from which we would get water for whatever was needed, were getting low, my dad would go fill them up. He would usually load both of the fifty-five gallon drums up by himself, onto a homemade trailer he had made, which he would pull with his pickup truck down by the Rio Grande River. Then he would fill both the drums with a bucket. That's where we got the water we used for drinking, cooking, washing the dishes or our clothes, and even taking a bath. And since we didn't have a hot water heater at the time, whenever we needed hot water, either my mom or my grandma would heat it up on the stove. It took a little longer, but that was okay; that taught us to have a little extra patience and the importance of planning for the future.

Like the good, old saying goes, "Don't put things off for tomorrow that you can do today." My dad knew that. And our water was the perfect example. It was simple; if he put off refilling those gallons, we could go thirsty and hungry, not have any clean dishes or clean clothes, and maybe even go around smelling kind of funky. That's why he kept a close eye on the water barrels all the time.

When it came to washing dishes, of course we needed some hot water, so whoever was going to wash the dishes at that time would have to go outside and get a bucketful of water and then pour about one-third of it into a pot. After we put it on the stove so it could get hot, then we'd pour it back into the bucket and mix it around real good. Since we didn't have a septic tank, we made sure there was an empty bucket underneath the sink at all times. That's where we had a straight drainpipe, and after the dishes were washed, we would take the bucket from underneath the sink and throw whatever was in there outside. That happened every time the dishes were going to get washed, and we didn't let the dishes get stacked up either.

When it was someone's turn to take a bath (which usually happened at my grandma's house), in this case mine, first, my mom or my grandma would get a bucketful of water. Then they would pour out about one-third of the bucket into a pot that got put on the stove. After the water got nice and hot, they would pour it back into the bucket. After mixing it up really well, it would be ready for me to take a bath. But I needed the big washtub. That's where I would stand up during my bath, so it would get put in the middle of the living room/bedroom area. Right next to that, I had my soap and the bucketful of warm water, with a small plastic cup so I could scoop up water from the bucket. First, I wet myself down. After that, I would soap myself up from head to toes. Then I would rinse all the soap off me. Afterward, I'd carefully step out of the tub and dry myself off. And finally after that, I would put my clean clothes on, while my mom or grandma would pour the water from the big tub back into the bucket and go throw it outside. One of them would also dry up any water that had gotten spilled down around where the big tub was. This was the drill every time anyone was going to take a bath, and no one ever made a big deal about having to wait for the water to get heated up on the stove.

Now when it came to the toilet, we had what is called an outhouse. The closest thing I can compare it with is a portable potty, except portable potties are moved quite often and outhouses are more stationary. The smell in it wasn't all that great, so you took care of business and got out of there as soon as possible. Plus, it had a nice, deep hole under it, about six feet deep. Children under ten years of age couldn't go to the outhouse by themselves, especially at nighttime, at least at our house. Usually the outhouses had two or three holes so people could sit down and take care of business. If a little person tried climbing up in order to sit down to take care of business, he or she could slip into one of the holes and hurt themselves— not to mention, the child could also drown in human fertilizer. That's why, to make things easier and safer in my case, either my mom or grandma would rip open a big grocery store paper bag, put it in the corner of the living room/bedroom area of my grandma's house, and I would take care of business there.

One day, my grandma noticed that our outhouse hole was getting almost full. So she told me we needed to dig another hole. She measured the outside of our outhouse with a broom handle. Then marked on the ground where she wanted the new one to go and started digging a hole slightly smaller than our outhouse. After she had dug the hole down about a foot on all four sides, she asked me, "Can you finish this hole that I started digging?"

I said, "Yeah grandma!"

"Make sure when you are digging not to go in or out on the sides. The hole needs to be dug straight down."

"Okay, Grandma."

I was only four and a half years old, but if my grandma asked me if I could help her, I felt good about that, so I got started on the digging right away. In the meanwhile, she had something to do inside the house. After a few minutes, two of my cousins who lived close by showed up.

"What are you doing?" asked Daniel, his hands on his hips and his eyes opened wide with curiosity.

"I'm helping my grandma dig this hole," I told him proudly.

"Can we help?" Fred asked.

"Sure," I said. "One of you guys grab a shovel and come in the hole with me because we all can't fit in here at the same time. You guys can take turns with the shovel. I was taking full advantage of my chance to direct. "Fred, you can come in here with me first, and then you can switch places with Daniel after a while."

After about an hour went by, my grandma came back out to see how I was doing on the hole. She said, "I see you have a little extra help now; that's good."

I explained to her that we were having a hard time shoveling the dirt out of the hole because it was getting deeper, and when we tried to shovel the dirt out, about half of it would land out of the hole and the other half was coming back down on top of us.

So Grandma tied a bucket at the end of a nice, long rope and gave us a good idea. She said, "The one who's outside of the hole can lower the bucket down, and the two of you who are digging in the hole can fill it up. Then the one out of the hole can pull up the bucket and dump out the dirt. That way, you'll finish a lot sooner, and it will be easier for you."

I said, "Thanks, Grandma."

After we got done digging the new hole, we had a nice dirt pile next to the old hole, and we used some of that dirt to fill up the old outhouse hole.

My grandma had intentionally measured the new hole close to the old one. That way we could kill two birds with one stone. I took charge of digging the hole and supervising my two cousins. That was another one of many confidence builders that were to come for me in the future.

In the meantime, the days seemed to be passing by way too quickly. Before we knew it, it was already time to go back up north and make some money. In other words, it was time to go to work. Some truck drivers spoke with some company owners they knew and got a contract for a certain amount of people to go work for them. Usually, a few of the truck drivers would be heading to wherever the work was, and those who didn't have a car or truck to drive could pick among them and get a ride in the back of one of those big trucks. The people who road in the back of the trucks would usually bring with them small kerosene stoves and pillows. The blankets, work clothes, normal everyday clothes, and anything foldable were put into a gigantic, homemade type of a pillowcase with drawstrings on one end to keep whatever was put in it from coming back out. That would also double as a mattress to either sit or lay on because, sometimes, the road trips would take a few days. The jobs could be as far away as South Texas to Washington State picking cherries or as near as South Texas to East or West Texas, only a few hours away, either cleaning some cotton fields or picking the cotton. Some people, who were blessed enough to have their own vehicles, would follow behind the truck drivers. My family was one of the blessed ones.

Sometimes the journey would take us to Indiana to pick asparagus. The owners of the asparagus fields had a number of houses where we could stay free of charge. That area was known as the Mexican camp. There was also a canning factory called the Sam's Pick near the camp where we all lived. My dad and some other people from the camp would work at night there when they weren't working out in the asparagus fields.

One night after working at the Sam's Pick Cannery, my dad heard through the grapevine that a little ways across the state line, on the Illinois side, the owners of a tree and shrub nursery were looking for some good workers. My dad found out where it was located. He also got the phone number to the office at the nursery and spoke with Thomas Stone, one of the owners, and found out that they needed five good men.

My dad talked to my grandpa and asked him, "What do you think about going to work at a tree nursery in Illinois?"

"I haven't ever worked at a tree nursery before," my grandpa said, "but we can go check it out."

My dad also talked to three of his close cousins, who worked at the same place. He asked them, "Do you guys want to go with me and my dad to check out some work at a tree and shrub nursery in the state of Illinois after we get done picking asparagus for the day?"

They all said, "Sure."

"Okay, we'll go see about that tomorrow."

The next day, after the men had finished picking asparagus, they all met by my dad's car, ready to work for a few more hours. The nursery was about an hour away from the camp, but the work would mean a little extra money. When they finally got to the nursery, Thomas explained to them what needed to get done. None of them had ever worked at a tree nursery before, so just about everything that needed to be done was new to them. But they did their very best. Plus, they were all light on their feet and fast learners.

After they'd spent a week going over there and working part-time Monday through Friday and all day Saturday, the two owners of the nursery were very impressed. They asked if the men were under contract at the asparagus fields.

The four men asked my dad to speak for them. So he answered and said, "We are under contract with the truck drivers picking asparagus. But the contract is going to be up soon, and it will still be spring."

"My brother William and I spoke," Thomas told them, "and we decided, if you men would like to come work for us, we will pay you one dollar an hour. We have some land in the little town of Pleasant Park with some houses on it where you and your families can live for free. You won't have to pay any rent, gas, electric, or water bills, as long as you are working for us."

Beto Jr. said, "We will talk it over, and I will let you know tomorrow." When they got home, the five men talked about how it would be nice to get paid by the hour instead of working under contract. All the other extras would make it seem as if they were getting paid a lot more than just one dollar an hour.

When they finally got back home, my dad told my mom and my grandpa told my grandma about everything Thomas and William had offered them. They all agreed the offer didn't sound bad. The other three men were single. They didn't have to talk it over with anybody else, and they all agreed it would be a good move.

The next day after they got done picking asparagus, the men went to work at the nursery. My dad spoke with Thomas. "We decided that, after we get done with the asparagus contract, we will move to Illinois and work at the nursery for you," he said.

In the meantime, they kept going to work at the nursery after they were done picking asparagus. This went on for a couple more weeks, and finally, the day came when the asparagus contract was done.

Like usual, the truck drivers took the people back to their homes in South Texas, and the people who drove their vehicles all followed behind—except for my dad's family, who had come with him in his car and his three cousins who all drove together in one car. We all headed toward Illinois to the little town of Pleasant Park. Once we got there, my dad called the nursery and spoke with Thomas. He told him, "We are all done working in Indiana, and we are at a phone booth by a Shell gas station in Pleasant Park."

"I know where that's at," Thomas replied. "I'll be there in a few minutes."

Sure enough, after a few minutes, Thomas showed up. He got out of his truck and walked over toward my dad's car. At the same time, my dad was getting out of his car and walking toward Thomas. They met between the car and the truck. Thomas said, "Nice to see you again. If you'll follow me, I'll show you where those houses are."

My dad went back toward his car and told his cousins what Thomas had said.

We went down two blocks, stopped at a stop sign, went straight for two more blocks to another stop sign, turned right, and went over some railroad tracks. After going around a curve and heading straight for a little ways, we turned left onto a gravel driveway. We came to an area that consisted of ten houses and a really nice, large two and a half-car garage, which would eventually end up being transformed in to a barrack for single men, its big garage door closed up. This also gave the men who would come to work without bringing their families a place to stay free of charge. I saw a couple great big Mulberry trees, and right next to them was some kind of a nut tree. It wasn't as tall as the Mulberry trees, but that was another tree to climb and explore, along with three nice-sized, little green apple trees and a big Mulberry bush toward the back of the camp. There was also a big yard with lots of green grass so we could play. I liked what I saw. I had a few action figures I would keep myself entertained with, and when it came to my action figures, I had an imagination and a half. My little sister had a few dolls she would pass the time with. At first it was only the two of us when it came to little people, "children."

One day, a nice lady knocked on our back door. She introduced herself, saying, "Hi, my name is Betty Smith. We're neighbors, and you can just call me Betty."

My mom said, "My name is Anna Zapata. You can call me Anna. Come on in."

"I can't stay long," Betty replied. "I just wanted to come over and introduce myself. I hope you like apple pie because I baked you one."

"Yes we do. Thank you."

"At our house, it's just my husband, Leroy and me, and we have two girls and two boys. We live in the house right behind your house and to the left. You're welcome to come on over anytime."

My mom said, "Thank you."

Betty added, "And if you need anything, just ask."

"Okay, are your children in school?"

"Yes, our oldest is Cherrie. She's in ninth grade, and Laurie, our other girl, is in seventh grade. Danny is our oldest boy. He's in fifth grade. And our youngest is Mack; he's in third grade. Do you have any children?"

"Yes, I have a son. His name is Johnny. He is four years old. I also have a daughter, Paula. She's one."

Betty asked, "When is Johnny's birthday?"

"The twenty-fourth of July."

"That's funny. Danny's birthday is on the twenty-sixth of July, and he's going to turn ten. I'll get you all the information about school and bring it over to you. What I do know is that, here in the Pleasant Park School, they only have first, second, and third grades. If you want to sign him up for kindergarten, he'll have to go to a city that's right next to us by the name of Kewanee. I'm sure they have kindergarten classes at George Washington Elementary School."

The closest I had ever been to a school classroom was when I went to Sunday school with my grandma at church, so I was definitely heading toward a new experience.

The next day was Thursday, and we found out that Betty was a woman of her word. At ten o'clock in the morning, she came over with all the information so I could get registered in school. After my mom read the papers Betty had brought over, she saw I wasn't too young and that me going to school wouldn't be a problem because of my birthday. She also saw where I would have to go in order to get picked up by the bus and at what time I would have to be there.

After my dad got home from work, she told him all about the information Betty had brought over. Remember, I was only four years old, and after my mom and dad had what I thought was way too short of a conversation about it they were in agreement; they would sign me up for kindergarten. They hadn't ever really taught me to be afraid of too many things in life. I was born on the twenty-fourth of July, 1961, and according to the school's handbook, I had a late birthday. But the way I saw it, it was perfect. It was in the middle of summer, and all the children in school had summer off for my birthday.

My mom and dad asked me if I was going to be afraid of riding the school bus over to the next town.

"No, I won't be afraid," I assured them.

They also told me that, at first, I wouldn't know any other children. My dad encouraged me by saying, "In the mornings, I will give you a ride to the bus stop on my way to work, and after a while, you will make a lot of new friends on the bus and at school. You can make friends with some little girls, and then you will have some girlfriends."

I said, "Okay, Dad."

From a very young age, I both heard and thought that having girls as friends would be all right; that was plural—girls as friends. At first, my desire to have multiple female friends was innocent, but with the years came the perversion of my mind.

Let me rewind for a moment. It is important for me to mention a short period during my life when I was a toddler. As the years went by, the family had been growing. Initially, it was just me. I was too small to remember the story I'm about to tell, but I thank my mom for telling me about this part of my life. The Lord blessed me, well, all of us for eight short months with a baby boy, who my parents named Reynaldo; he was called Rey for short. His departure came as a devastating surprise, like a thief in the night, especially because, nothing was visibly wrong with him. My mom, as she did every other morning, went to his crib to check on him. It was abnormal for him to stay sleeping and be extra quiet like he was. To her shock, she found his little, cold, lifeless body. At that time, not much was known about crib death.

Now that's something no mother should ever have to experience. The whole family was caught off guard; they were all shocked at the news. My mom especially was devastated, but with time and lots of prayer, life got better. The void that was left from my baby brother's absence was slowly but surely smoothed over by the birth of a beautiful little baby girl. My parents named her Paula. That wasn't even half of all the children the Lord would eventually bless my mom and dad with. After Paula was born, the family kept on growing, with six more children, until 1978.

Altogether, we were a total of eight alive here on earth and one alive in heaven waiting for the rest of us. I thank God for the parents he gave me, and by parents I'm also including my grandparents because they played a big part in my growing up; well actually, they did for all of us Zapata children. Since I was the oldest, I had the privilege of being instructed the longest. I don't ever remember hearing, not even once, just give up, that's impossible, or you'll be wasting your time by trying. On the contrary, what I always remember hearing is, where there's a will, there's a way.

CHAPTER 3

EXCEEDING ABUNDANTLY ABOVE MY IMAGINATION

The first year we moved to Illinois, my dad and grandpa were the only ones from our family who had a job at the nursery. I thought the camp was nice and big. I really liked climbing the different kinds of trees I saw there, especially the two little green apple trees toward the front of the camp. Another one for me to climb was toward the middle of the camp. That one had a branch that was perfect for a swing. Its apples weren't as good as those from the other two, but it was a challenge to climb in order to tie a rope for a swing. My little sister and I were the only little people that first year. Don't get me wrong, I love my little sister, but she just wasn't a boy. I thank God for the following year.

When we all had arrived at the camp that year, it was early springtime 1967. My mom and dad had just been blessed with another perfectly healthy baby boy a couple of months before we got there. They named him Roman. I didn't ever ask my dad who was going to work with him that year at the nursery. That wasn't that important to me. The way I figured things, that was his business.

I didn't know this particular new family that had driven up with us. Even though they also lived in the same little town of Las Palomas, I don't remember ever going over to their house and visiting. I would find out later that we were actually related. The new family consisted of my uncle Joel; his wife Yolanda; and their son, who would later become my best friend, Rodolfo. Everybody just called him Rudy. I didn't know the major role they would play in my life in the near future. They started coming up to Illinois every year with us after that, and my uncle and aunt both eventually worked at the nursery. My cousin and I were about six months apart in age. We were together just about all the time. Some of the people who didn't really know us at first would ask us if we were brothers. We would always say, "No, we're just cousins."

Four years later, my mom and dad were blessed with two more boys. The first one they named Jorge, and the second one Francisco, like my dad's brother. We just called him Rico for short.

At first glance, 1971 seemed to be a not-so-good year. That was the year my Grandpa Zapata got pretty sick and ended up in the hospital. Then the doctors transferred him to a second hospital, which was a little farther away in Plainfield Illinois. I remember one Saturday my dad said, "Let's go to the Plainfield Hospital and see your grandpa."

The whole family got in my dad's truck, and we made the hour and a half-drive southwest of where we lived. Once we found out what room my grandpa was in, my dad went to his room, and with a little help, my grandpa was able to sit in a wheelchair. My dad pushed him in the wheelchair by the lobby where the rest of us were waiting for him. We all followed behind them outside to this place where there was a lot of nice, green grass underneath a big shade tree. That way, we could spend some time with him. We had taken some food and pop to drink, so we could have a picnic and take some pictures with him. We had a really nice time that day.

On the way back home, my dad stopped at a little drugstore in the small town of Cedarville. He needed to buy some Polaroid film for his camera because he had used it all up at the hospital when we were taking pictures with my grandpa. I was in the back of the truck with two of my little brothers. When he parked in the front parking lot, I stood up. My dad asked me, "Do you want to come inside with me?"

I said, "Yeah, Dad."

The drugstore wasn't very big, so I went looking around all over and found where they had some toys. I saw this nice-looking airplane that had a handheld remote control. It could fly by itself, and I really liked the way it looked. I didn't say anything to my dad right away. He found the camera film and paid for it, and then he said. "Come on. Let's go." We got back in the truck and continued home.

When we finally got home, I kept on thinking about the airplane I had seen. I told him, "I saw an airplane at the drugstore when we stopped to get the film, and I thought it looked real nice, Dad."

He asked me, "Why didn't you tell me that you liked it when we were at the drugstore?"

"I thought you were in a hurry."

Long story short, my dad said, "Come on. Let's go get it."

When we got to the drugstore, he said, "Go get it, so I can pay for it."

I was just telling him about the airplane, I didn't really think he would drive all the way back and buy it for me because it was a couple of towns away.

They eventually found out my grandpa was seriously ill, and he didn't ever walk out of that hospital. He went to heaven that year.

It was a good thing that, when we were migrating back and forth from South Texas to the northeast part of Illinois, my dad had kept in contact with Thomas, one of the owners of the Kewanee Nursery. Thomas would let my dad know how many people they needed to start out with in the springtime.

As time had been passing by, my dad's name began to get well known; people knew there was a nursery in Kewanee, Illinois, and the man to talk with if you wanted to work starting in the springtime would be young Beto Zapata. He was the main boss there. If the nursery had all the people it needed at the time, and people still kept on coming in search of work, my dad would have them write down their names and the telephone number where they could be reached. Later on, if the nursery needed more people, he would give them a call so they could come and work. Everybody who knew him agreed he was a good, fair man who would give you a hand and help you out in any way he could.

But you didn't ever want to mistake his meekness for weakness. A wise man once said, "For every action, there's a reaction."

My grandma would take us Zapata children to church every Sunday, depending on our age and how well we listened to her. But we weren't ever really taught about stranger danger, so I thought everybody was like my mom and dad, or any of our close relatives.

As my cousin and I were getting older, our parents started trusting us and giving us more freedom to wander around the camp by ourselves, which was not the best thing to do in our case. On one particular day, my cousin and I had been running around all over the camp like a couple of normal nine- and ten-year-olds. Then we decided to go into the barracks and say hi to a couple of the men who we knew and considered friends. The women from the camp or any other respectable females would never even think of going in there. Nor could little children go in there either, so to us, venturing into the barracks that first day meant we weren't little children anymore. Our moms would still tell us not to go into the barracks because most of the men who lived there were young, single, and a lot older than us. They just didn't think that was a good environment for us, and of course they were right.

But we didn't listen. Our taste for the lifestyle we were introduced to at the barracks started out gradually. First of all, before visiting the barracks, my cousin and I hadn't ever seen or even heard of anything close to a pornographic magazine before. But that didn't last long. Our family didn't know most of the men who ended up living in the barracks before they came there. My dad just knew about the people through other people who had worked at the nursery before them. Rudy and I started going to the barracks, where we had gotten our first eyeful, more often. Almost all of the young men would bring some magazines with them from wherever they'd came. After they had gotten settled in and worked at least a couple of weeks, they would add to their collection of magazines—the kind that most young, single guys read, or mostly look at. And I'm not talking about *Popular Mechanics* either. I heard, and it was explained to me, that there was nothing wrong with having more than just one girlfriend. As a matter of fact, I would get asked, "Do you mean to tell me that you only have one girlfriend?"

I only had friends who were girls, so I told them, "I have a bunch of girlfriends," which was true but not the way they meant it.

With time, my blister had become a callous, in a matter of speaking. The way I thought was, *If anyone has only one girlfriend, that isn't normal, and there is something definitely wrong with that picture.*

The Lord continued to show me his love and grace through my parents. He surprised me big-time in a way I couldn't have even imagined. Between my mom and dad, they looked in the newspaper, and found a 1969 Honda 300 motorcycle for a nice, low price. My dad called the seller and got the directions to his house. He told me to come with them, so he could go look at a motorcycle. I thought, *Cool, my dad's looking for a motorcycle.*

When we got there, my dad and I got out of the car while my mom waited for us. We started walking toward the house, and the man must have been waiting for us or looking out of his window, maybe both. He was coming out of his house and said, "Hi, are you here about the motorcycle?"

My dad said, "Yeah."

"My name is Jimmy," the man told him. "She's over here."

He walked toward his garage, waving us over. He slid open a big, heavy-looking door, and there in front of us was a not-so-modern-looking but nice and clean motorcycle with a black and white paint job and two chrome mufflers going back. I thought, *That motorcycle looks different than all of the other motorcycles I've seen before.* I was looking it over from all sides. I thought, *It looks nice, but I haven't ever heard of or seen a Honda 300 motorcycle before.* It reminded me of the motorcycle the Fonz from *Happy Days* would ride.

After that is when the big surprise came for me. My dad asked me, "Do you like it?"

I said, "Yeah, Dad, it looks real nice."

"Get on it," my dad said, his tone casual.

So I did, and I was still thinking, *Why does he want me to get on it if it's for him?* But I didn't hesitate. I jumped on it right away. He asked me, "Can you hold it up?"

I said, "Yeah, Dad."

"Let me see you straighten it up."

It was heavy, and I had to go from the left side to the right side on the tip of my toes, but I could hold it up. The man had the keys in his pocket. As he was taking them out he said, "Let me start her up for you, so you can hear how she sounds."

I got off, and he got on and put the key in the ignition switch, located on the left side by where the motor was, and turned the key looking up. He squeezed the clutch and pressed on a little black button that was located next to the gas throttle, while at the same time twisting the gas throttle a little, and it started right away. He revved it up a few times and kept it running for a couple more seconds. Then he said, "Here's the kill switch to turn it off. You can reach both the kill switch and the starter button with your thumb easily. It has an electric starter right here on the handlebars, or you can use the kick-starter. It also has a regular kickstand, or you can use the other one that's located right underneath it. Here, let me show you. First you step on this right here, then you grab it from this handle and you pull up and back on the motorcycle like this. The ground underneath it must be flat and hard, but the whole bike will be in the air. You can teeter-totter the bike and let either the front tire or the back tire touch the ground. It comes in handy if you need to work on the bike. If you want to get it off this kickstand and you're sitting on it, you just push it forward a little like this." As he put it back on its side kickstand and got off he said, "Here, let me show you this." He took the key out of the ignition and put the same key into a keyhole on the right side by the motorcycle's seat. He turned it and showed us that the seat could open up. He also showed us an owner's manual underneath there and a couple of hooks where you could hang your motorcycle helmets on. If you closed the seat, it would lock; it was safer to put your helmets there than to just leave them somewhere on top of the motorcycle. He also showed us another compartment located around the middle of the motorcycle close to the engine. You could access the compartment by taking a black, plastic cover off either side. In it were about seven tools rolled up in a little, black plastic pouch in case of an emergency; that way you'd have something to work with.

He said, “Oh and before I forget, let me show you this one last thing. If you're going to park the bike somewhere and you want to lock the handlebars with the front tire pointing sideways, just take the key and put it in this here spot. It's straight in the middle of the handlebars; push it in while turning it to the left at the same time. It'll be locked that way until you choose to unlock it. Well that's it; do you have any other questions for me?”

“No.” My dad looked at the man and said, “Here's the money.” The man said, “Okay, I'll go get the title.”

When he came back, he had the title already signed. They made an exchange of the title for the money. The man counted the money and said, “Thank you,” while my dad looked the title over, replying simply, “Yeah.” He has always been a man of few words. Then my dad told me to go in the car with my mom and he would see us at home.

After I got in the car, I told my mom what dad had said and then we headed home. My dad arrived a few seconds after my mom and I got home. He pulled in next to a little pine tree that was in our front yard and then he turned the motorcycle off, put the side kickstand on, and got off the motorcycle. He said, “Get on it and take it for a ride in the back of the camp.”

I climbed on and said, “Okay.”

“First, you always make sure that it's in neutral, which it is. You can tell by rocking it back and forth. Next squeeze the clutch in; it's the handle in front of your left hand,” he instructed. “Now with your left foot, tap that little lever down; did you feel that?”

“Yes.”

“Those are your gears. Now it's in first gear. Now stick the tip of your shoe underneath that little lever and move it up; did you feel that?”

“Yes.”

“You just put it back in neutral. Now let go of the clutch and turn the key on. When it's in neutral, you don't need the clutch squeezed in to turn the motorcycle on.”

I said, “Okay.”

He told me, "Now straighten it up and take the kickstand off. Push that little, black button with your right thumb to turn it on and twist the throttle a little at the same time."

I did what my dad said, and sure enough, it started up right away. I had twisted the throttle and given it too much gas, but being that it was my first time, I thought, *That's okay. I'll know better the next time.*

My dad said, "Squeeze the clutch in and tap that little lever down with your foot. Remember, those are your gears, and you always need to squeeze the clutch in before messing with your gears. Now slowly let go of the clutch and give it a little gas at the same time."

Since it was my first time ever trying to ride a motorcycle, I let go of the clutch too quickly, and the motorcycle stalled on me.

My dad said, "That's okay; try it again."

So I did the same thing about three more times. Finally, I was able to get it going, only in first gear, but I was having fun. I followed the driveway toward the back of the camp and kept going straight onto the grassy area that was by the railroad tracks. There was a space back there going north and south about the size of three city blocks, so I had plenty of room to practice riding the motorcycle. My dad walked back there and was watching me ride back and forth. He yelled at me one of those times I was riding by him and said, "Squeeze the clutch in and with your left foot move that little lever up past neutral and put it in second gear, so you can go faster!"

I yelled back, "Okay, Dad!"

First gear was nice, but second gear was even better.

Once my dad heard the motorcycle engine sound like I needed to shift again, he motioned me to stop. Before I reached the spot where he was, he reminded me, "Make sure you always squeeze the clutch in before stopping when it's in gear."

I said, "Okay, Dad."

"Remember, you are in second gear, so before you take off again, you need to tap it back down past neutral and into first gear with the clutch squeezed in, so you don't strip your gears. That way, when you are going to start moving again, it won't turn off on you. When you are moving, listen to the motor. When it sounds all revved up like it needs to burp, it's time to shift into the next gear. And don't forget to keep looking at the rpm gauge every once and a while. You want to make sure you don't ever rev the motor up until it gets into the red zone and keep it there, or you can blow the engine."

One more thing he reminded me was, "It has a total of four gears besides neutral."

Now that was a lot for me to remember, but what made it sound even sweeter was hearing my dad say, "You have to take good care of it because it's yours."

I remember hearing someone say once, "To whom much is given, much is required." When my dad said the motorcycle was mine, at that exact time, much had just been given to me, so that meant much was about to be required of me. I will have to admit, when my dad said I had to take good care of it because it was mine, I was caught off guard for a minute or two. But that was all right. Not once did I ever think, *Oh no, that's too much for me. I don't deserve that.* Forget that noise; I just thought, *Yes*! And I said, "Thank you, thank you, thank you, Dad!"

Slowly but surely, with a little time and a lot of patience, I learned how to use the clutch and get the motorcycle moving from a complete standstill without it stalling on me. I also learned how to shift gears up and down the right and proper way, nice and smooth. The house we lived in had a cement porch floor with one step up. My grandma told me to find a small board. The one I found was around twenty inches long by about seven inches wide. I put it from the ground to the porch, like a little ramp, in order to get the motorcycle up and into the porch to keep it out of the rain or snow. I also used the board to drive the motorcycle off the porch whenever I felt like riding around. That was about every day; as long as it wasn't raining or snowing too hard, I would be on the motorcycle having fun. Just thinking about how I was on my very own motorcycle and I was only ten brought a big smile to my face.

If I wasn't using the board, I would always put it on the porch, right next to the motorcycle's front tire. That way, I always knew where it was when I needed it again. I learned that from my Grandma Zapata, and it does make a lot of sense.

It didn't take me too long before I felt really comfortable on the motorcycle, and riding it felt like second nature to me. After three short weeks, I was trying to do some of the moves on my motorcycle that I had previously learned how to do on my three-speed bike, which my dad had also bought me. I discovered that I could have a lot more fun on the motorcycle than I'd ever had on my bike. I was constantly looking for bumps or dips so I could pop some kind of a wheelie; they weren't always pretty, especially in the beginning. At first, I could only get the front tire about three inches off the ground. But with time, I learned to raise it two to three feet into the air, and that was on a Honda 300, a heavy street bike. I discovered that, by finding a bump or dip and then giving it a little extra gas while simultaneously pulling back on the handlebars, I'd get the front tire off the ground every time. I also learned how to make what's called a donut with the back tire by first stopping the motorcycle and making sure it was in first gear. Then I'd put my left foot down and lean the motorcycle slightly to my left, while at the same time sharply turning my front tire also to the left. Then I'd give it a little extra gas and let go of the clutch all of a sudden, keeping my front tire constantly turned while the back tire was peeling out, and the dirt, grass, and whatever else was in the back tire's way got thrown a good ten feet away. The result was a nice, smooth, round-looking shape on the ground called a donut. I eventually learned how to do it on the right side also.

When I first learned how to make a donut, I could only do it when the ground was wet, such as after a light shower. If it was wintertime and there was a little snow on the ground, that would also help me out because the motorcycle was pretty heavy. Now that's what I called having fun.

After about four more years had gone by, I totally got the hang of the motorcycle, and I was able to maneuver it the way I wanted, when I wanted.

I started to notice—but I thought it was because I was growing up and not because of the company I chose to keep—that my ways of acting, thinking, and speaking had become more and more polluted. And that was just the beginning.

I couldn't see it at the time, but the Lord continued to show me His love and big-time blessings. First, through my parents, He gave me another beautiful little sister, named Rachel, and another little brother, Ramiro.

One Saturday morning, my dad said, "Hey, Johnny, come with your mom and me to the Honda shop in Kewanee."

I said, "Okay, Dad."

We had been by the shop many times before, but we hadn't ever stopped in. I always liked going with my dad anywhere and everywhere. I didn't know if he needed my help to do something or what. All I knew is my dad had asked me to go with him, and I was going to have a good time.

The shop was about seven miles away from our house, and when we got there, I started looking around at all the shiny, new motorcycles. The shop had a wide variety of bikes, from the big Gold Wing street bikes on down, as well as some super tough-looking dirt bikes with big, knobby tires. They reminded me of gigantic grasshoppers. Everything looked super tall on them; the ones with 350, 250, and 150 motors on them looked like they could easily climb up a telephone pole.

I also saw some little bitty dirt bikes that I hadn't ever seen before. I didn't even know they made dirt bikes that small. I thought, *These little motorcycles sure do look cute.* I didn't know where to start looking. There were all different sizes to look at, and they all looked nice to me.

Then I noticed that, on one of the walls, the shop had on display everything you could think of when it came to motorcycles, from motorcycle helmets to dirt bike riding boots and everything in between. I could have spent hours looking around in there and never have gotten bored. The shop had two checkout counters—one in the front and the other in the back. Both of them had see-through glass tops on the side of the cash registers with two levels full of rings, bracelets, necklaces, earrings, motocross gloves, thin-skinned motorcycle riding gloves, and a lot of other things.

My dad called me over to a particular motorcycle he was looking at; it was a Honda XL 250. I found out later on the letters XL meant the motorcycle could be ridden on trails, as well as on the street legally, if you had a driver's license for it. I didn't really know there were motorcycles made for street and trail purposes, or what I thought was for really having fun. My dad asked me, "What do you think about this bike?"

I said, "I think it looks real nice, Dad."

He told me to get on it. I straddled it in a New York second. He said, "If you like it, I'll buy it for you, and we'll take it home right now."

I said, "Okay, Dad. I like it a lot."

He told me to go find a salesman.

As I was getting off the bike, a salesman was approaching us. He said, "You and that bike look good together."

I said, "Thanks."

The salesman did his job and told us all about the motorcycle without knowing that my dad had already made up his mind to buy it for me.

When I was on the motorcycle, I would have to be on the tip of my toes, but I was used to that because of my first motorcycle, so it didn't really bother me. After my dad bought the motorcycle for me, he rode it home and parked it in our front yard. I got on it right away. Since I'd had a lot of fun learning how to pop wheelies and make donuts on that big 300 Honda motorcycle, this new XL 250 felt really light in my hands. So everything I'd learned with the other motorcycle I was going to be able to do even more easily with this one.

I had been blessed to be able to work since before I turned thirteen. Sometimes, my dad would take us Zapata children, well, the whole family really, to pick tomatoes or walk bean fields, and that was after he got off work at the nursery. That's when he would take us for a few hours or maybe even on the weekends. That way, we could learn how to work and, at the same time, to not be afraid of sweating a little.

At the age of thirteen, I worked as a helper dealing with little people, *children* from five to ten year olds, for the Illinois Mexican Laborers Association. When we got paid there, it was always by check every two weeks, and I would get my paycheck in a sealed envelope. I wouldn't even open it. I would just hand it over to my dad. I only worked there for a couple of years, and that was during our summer vacations. I have some good memories from helping out there, while at the same time learning how to work for a paycheck.

When I was fifteen years old, my dad told me I should ask William, one of the owners of the Kewanee Nursery, for a job and tell him that I would work wherever he needed me. The day my dad told me this was a Sunday.

So on Monday, right after school, I hurried home, changed my clothes, and told my mom, "I'm going to the nursery on my motorcycle to ask for a job. I'll be back later."

She told me, "Be careful and don't ride the motorcycle in town." I said, "Okay, Mom. I'll be back later."

I rode down the railroad tracks and through one side of our park and then made my way across a bridge that divides our two parks. I had both of my feet dangling down stepping on the road, pretending to walk the motorcycle across the bridge, while still driving it. When I got to the other side, I took a good look in front of me and then looked in my rearview mirrors as I got on the right side of the road. I rode south for a couple of miles. And just as if I had made an appointment with him, I ran into William, who had gotten out of his truck to look over some plants. I thought, *For sure I will have to go to the main office to speak with William.* But I ran into him a good half mile before the main office building.

I rode up on my motorcycle, got off, and said, "Hi, William. How have you been doing?"

He said, "Okay. How about you?"

"I've been fine, thank you. I'm looking for a job after school. Do you have anything that you need help with?"

"Come by tomorrow. I'm sure we could find something for you to do."

"Thank you, William. I have to go now. I'll see you tomorrow."

When I got home, I told my mom, "I spoke with William, and he said I could start working at the nursery tomorrow after school."

When my dad got home that day, he said, "I was talking with William, and he told me that Johnny had stopped by and asked for a job after school. He asked me how old Johnny was. I told him he is fifteen years old."

William had said, "We can't have him working out in the fields; our insurance won't cover him because of his age. I thought he was sixteen."

The next day after school, I went home and changed my clothes. I told my mom and grandma, "I'll see you later. I'm going to work." I jumped on my motorcycle, and I was off.

Once I was at the nursery, I saw William and my dad talking, so I went over by them.

William asked me, "Are you ready to work?" I said, "I sure am."

"Go with your dad, and he will show you what to do," he told me.

My dad walked me toward the back by one of the buildings and told me to clean some tin plates, a whole bunch of them, with a wire brush so they would be ready for the budding season in spring. The job was outside underneath a big shade tree, and it seemed kind of boring to me. But after my dad explained the conversation he had with William about the insurance not covering me, I thought, *Well, at least it's not a hard job.*

After a month had gone by, another Friday came, and at the end of the workday, I punched my time card like I had all of the other days. When I saw my dad, I said, "Hi, Dad!"

He said, "Hi!" He had a bunch of checks in his hand to pass out to the workers.

I told him, "I'll see you at home, Dad." He said, "Okay."

Not once did I say, "I worked all week. Where's my paycheck, Dad?" One month before my sixteenth birthday, my dad surprised me once again. I was coming out of our house and onto our porch to get on my motorcycle and drive it around for a little while. I noticed the motorcycle wasn't where I had parked it last, and at that precise moment, my dad was driving up in the yard on a smaller-looking motorcycle, like the ones we had seen before at the Honda shop. It looked a little smaller in the motor department, but that was okay; it was a shiny, new motorcycle. I said, "Hi, Dad."

He said, "Hi. I got you this motorcycle with a smaller-sized motor so that, when you get your license, you can drive around on it legally, or in the car you have."

I really liked the feeling I got when I was driving that new motorcycle—well, really whenever I got anything new. It may have been used, but if it was new to me, I just liked the feeling. Things seemed to be getting better and better for me. Whenever I thought things couldn't get any sweeter, *BAM!* I would get another big surprise.

Two weeks passed by. One Saturday morning, I had been out thoroughly enjoying myself riding around on my new XL 125. It seemed like any other day in the middle of summertime. My dad had gone out. I didn't know or ask where. To my pleasant surprise, he drove onto our front yard in a light yellow, but nice-looking car. He said, "I was driving past the Chevy dealer on my way into Kewanee. I had bought a few other cars there before, so they already knew me. When I saw the Nova, I immediately stopped and asked about it." He told the salesman, "I was looking for a car for my son, who is about to turn sixteen."

The salesman did his job and told him all about the car. He added, "This would be a perfect car for a sixteen year-old."

My dad told him, "I will go home and bring my son so he can see the car."

That's when the man told him, "Wait for me here; I'll be right back." He came back right away. "I spoke with my supervisor, and he said to let you take the car and show it to your son. Here are the keys to the car," he said, handing them to my dad. "My supervisor said you've bought a few cars from us before. We know and trust you, Mr. Zapata. Drive the car home and show it to your son. If he likes it, we'll take it from there."

When I'd first seen the car, I had no idea why he wanted me to check it out. I thought, *Cool, my dad is going to buy another car.*

But then he said, "Get close to it and look it over."

I was looking inside, and he said, "Follow me back here." He walked to the back of the car with the keys in his hand. He showed me how it didn't have a trunk, but it did have an area behind the backseat that could be used in place of a trunk. That area was all carpeted. It reminded me of my dad's 1976 Chevy custom Van. The back window was part of the trunk, so when he opened what should be the trunk, the back window also came up. I guess that's why they called it a hatchback.

I hadn't ever seen a car that could do that before. I said, "Wow, that's cool, Dad!"

But the surprise for me came when he asked me, "Do you like it?" I said, "Yeah, Dad!"

"The color isn't real important; you can change that pretty easy. It starts with no hesitation, and the motor's clean. I checked the oil and the tailpipe, and they're both clean. The transmission oil is clean. I checked the water in the radiator, and it has a solid body. It rides real nice and smooth going down the road. It's clean inside and out."

Again I said, "Cool, Dad! I like it a lot."

So he said, "Okay, I'll drive the car back to the dealer, sign the papers, and pay for the car. I'll take your mom with me, so she can drive the van back."

When my parents got back, I had my very own first car before I'd even turned sixteen. I didn't ever think I was spoiled. I was just blessed big-time. My dad would always buy me things and sometimes without me even asking. He would just surprise me all of a sudden, and many of the times, the surprises were brand spanking new. In addition, he gave me a ten-dollar allowance each week. As far as I was concerned, I had it made in the shade.

Thanks to hindsight, I was able to see that, because of the people I chose to hang around with, I had slowly but surely started to get a perverted and wicked mind that I couldn't understand. But God still showed me His love and grace through my parents.

CHAPTER 4

DESPERATE TIMES CALL FOR DESPERATE MEASURES

It was a Friday and a summer evening. After working all week, I was ready to go out on the town, get wild, and have some fun. To start out with, I was sixteen years old, and with a car that had a Holly 4 barrel carburetor. It had some Gabriel Hijackers air-adjustable shock absorbers. I had to get four-inch spacers on my rear hubs so the nice, big, fat, tires could fit on the car that my dad had helped me get. They were used, but they were mine. All of those things together were the perfect combination for a good time.

I had been working at the Kewanee Nursery all summer and had made a lot of friends—especially with the young men who were around my age. I got along with two of the guys particularly well. The three of us would spend a lot of time together at work and after work. Falcon and Mr. Big Stuff were the nicknames my two friends were known by. Once the weekend rolled around, my partying buddies and I were ready for some action. I got invited to a few different parties that were going down on the weekend. So of course, I brought my two friends with me. They didn't speak English all that well, but that was okay with me. Wherever we went, we always had a good time. Sometimes, we would be the only three Mexicans at the party—well actually, I'm a Mexican American, but we would be the only three dark-skinned young men there. I didn't ever feel embarrassed or out of place anywhere I went. I wasn't ever taught that way. As long as I acted right and respected people, I always got the same back in return. That's the way I was taught.

There was a moment when I stopped hanging around the guys for a little while, but I had a good, legitimate reason, and that was *LOVE*. Let me be the one to tell you, there was a sweet, Mexican American, hot-looking, beautiful young lady who I had seen around the camp a couple of times before. I had my eye on her from the very first time I saw her. In my opinion, she had the curves of a 1971 Corvette Stingray convertible and the front bumper of a 1941 Cadillac Series 62 convertible sedan. Whoa, sweet mama!

One day, I saw that her brother-in-law's bronco was over at my Uncle Joel's house, so I said to myself, *I think I'll go see what Rudy is going to do today.* I went over to his house and knocked on the front door. When my aunt Yolanda answered the door, I asked, "Is Rudy here?"

She said, "Yes. Come in; he's in his bedroom."

I asked Rudy about the girl and her family. He said, "They're friends of my mom and dad."

I said, "Oh, that's cool. Can you go out?"

"Yeah, let's go."

As we were going from his bedroom and through the living room, where she was sitting on the sofa, Rudy said, "Mary, this is my cousin, Johnny."

I said, "Hi."

I finally got to meet and talk to her, though not in the way I would have liked to. It was just a simple hi and bye, which was nice. But I wanted to have a one-on-one talk with her, just the two of us.

Her sister and my aunt hooked her up with someone else, but that didn't last long, thank God! I felt I had to wiggle my way in close to her somehow. During the time my aunt and her sister were playing matchmakers, I had gotten introduced to a girl by the name of Jenny. I found out that she and the girl who had caught my eye were friends. So I asked Jenny, "Will you be my girlfriend?" And she said, "Yeah."

Her parents would let me come over to their house so I could spend time with her. That wasn't quite what made my day; and I wasn't seeing what I really wanted to see. That was me getting closer to the only sweet, young Latin girl worth looking at in the whole county, according to me, by the name of Maria. Everybody just called her Mary. I know that wasn't the nicest thing to do, but you know how that old saying goes—"desperate times call for desperate measures."

I couldn't explain the feeling that I had at the time. But usually I would find trying to juggle a couple of girls at the same time (especially if they knew each other) challenging. And I had been raised thinking it was cool to have at least a couple of girlfriends at the same time—as long as I told the girls the right lies and they believed me. I felt something different this time—something that I hadn't ever felt before—from the very first time I saw Mary. I wanted to be the only one for her, and I wanted her to be the only one for me. I didn't know exactly how I was going to pull it off, but I knew somehow, I just had to make it happen.

What I didn't know, and I still believe to this day, is that God Almighty had picked her out especially for me. I was able to see clearly with time that we were meant for each other. I know that sounds like a cliché, but God knew what I didn't, and that was what the future had in store for me.

In the meantime, Jenny and Mary were planning a party for three, hopefully four teenagers at Jenny's house. Her parents were going to be there but in another part of the house, in order to make us feel like we were all alone in the house. I, as usual, was thinking like a typical teenage boy, otherwise known as a "hound dog," and I usually felt an urge to merge. You know how those out-of-control teenage hormones are.

I found it strange and not like me at all when I asked Jenny, "Is it okay with Mary's mom for her to be partying like that?"

Jenny said, "It's not like we're going to be getting buck wild and crazy. My mom and dad are going to be in the next room."

The reason why I asked was I knew how strict Mary's parents were with her. That was one of the things that attracted me to her. From what I heard, she was different from all the other girls I had known before. She had been raised the traditional South Texas way—without as much freedom to get into mischief, unlike most of the other girls I knew.

As the day of the party was getting closer, Jenny asked me, "Do you think your cousin, Rudy, would like to come to the party? That way, Rudy and Mary can have a chance to check each other out and see if anything serious can come out of it."

I had mixed emotions about that idea. I thought, *That's great. I'll be there, and so will Mary.* But the part about Mary checking Rudy out I wasn't too crazy about.

The day of the party finally arrived. My cousin and I were taking a last look in the mirror before jumping in my car and heading toward the little town of St. Austin. We were both feeling a little anxious to get to the party. Jenny lived in a two-story, decent-sized house at the end of a new subdivision. Mary and her mom were staying with her older sister, Julia, and her family, who lived in the house right next to Jenny's. The party was supposed to start at seven in the evening. When we pulled up in the driveway, it was a little after seven. The weather that evening was perfect. It wasn't raining. It wasn't too hot or humid. It was just right. We could see both of the girls, as they were looking out from a corner of the living room picture window.

We got out of the car, walked to the door, and rang the doorbell. Both of the girls answered the door and said, "Come in."

Jenny introduced herself to my cousin and added, "This is my friend, Mary." She looked at me and Rudy and asked, "Do you guys want something to drink? We have Pepsi or 7 Up, and we have a few different kinds of chips too."

We all sat down at a table, and Jenny, of course, sat next to me on one side while Mary and Rudy sat on the other side. After a few minutes went by, and everybody started to loosen up a little, Jenny leaned over and whispered in my ear, "It was good that your cousin decided to come with you so Mary could have someone here for her."

When she said that, what immediately came to my mind was, *So what am I, chopped liver? I'm here for her!*

We all had a great time that night. We talked, laughed, and drank some pop; we ate pretzels, potato chips, and my favorite, Doritos. I got to talk with Mary more than I had ever spoken with her before. I don't know about anybody else, but I felt super great that night.

After I had been home for a little while, Jenny called me and said, "You sure did have a lot to talk about with Mary tonight."

I said, "I wanted her to feel comfortable, and it was just regular talk. I talked with everybody."

"That's why you brought Rudy, so he could talk with her and keep her company," she said, her pitch getting louder and higher.

I asked, "Did Mary say anything about tonight?"

"Why don't you ask her yourself," she said and apparently handed Mary the phone.

I said, "Hello … hello …"

I heard a soft, gentle, "Hi. I don't want to be the cause of any trouble between the two of you."

"There's no trouble. Jenny just got angry because I said a few words to you, but if she wants to be angry, that's cool with me. Don't let that make you feel bad. Well, I have to go now, but maybe we'll talk tomorrow. You have a good night."

The next day around ten o'clock in the morning, the phone in the living room rang. I was in the kitchen and, at that precise moment, walking toward the living room, so I answered the phone and recognized that soft, gentle voice again. "Hello," she said.

I said, "Mary!"

"I don't want you to get the wrong idea. My reason for calling is that I don't want you and Jenny getting angry at each other." I could hear the sincerity in her voice.

"That's okay if you called," I said. As we talked, I paced slowly back and forth holding the phone in my right hand and twirling the cord with my left index finger.

"I don't usually do things like this," she told me, sounding a little embarrassed.

I said, "Not that I mind, but how did you get my number?" I motioned with my finger across my lips to my little brothers Rico and Ramiro to be quiet because they were running through the living room yelling at each other.

"Your dad and my brother-in-law, Alex, have to talk to each other about work or workers sometimes. So he has your dad's number here. And my sister helped me get it. I hope you don't mind."

I closed my left fist tightly and pulled my arm back while picking my left knee up and silently mouthed the word, *Yes*! I said, "No, not at all, but I can't talk to you how I would like to on this line. Let me give you my number, and you can call me back, if that's okay with you."

"Let me talk with my sister," she said. I could hear the phone being muffled on the other end.

After she got back to the phone, she said, "Why don't I just give you my number, and you can call me back."

With a big grin on my face, I said, "Great! That will work too." She asked, "Are you ready?" She sounded happy to me.

As I scrambled around, I said, "No, wait a minute. Let me get a piece of paper and something to write with. All right, go ahead and give me your number."

As soon as I got her number, I ran up the stairs and into my room, shut the door, and locked it. I dialed her number and laid back on my bed, totally relaxed. When she answered the phone, I said, "Hi, did you have a good time last night?"

She said, "Yes, I enjoyed myself, but I didn't want to start any trouble between Jenny and you."

"You didn't start any trouble. To be real honest with you, the one I really wanted to be with last night was you."

"You're going out with Jenny, and she's my friend," she said.

"I can take care of that right away. Let me call you back a little later," I said and then hung up.

I called up Jenny and told her I wanted to break up because I liked somebody else.

She said, "Wait a minute. Let's talk this over. Why don't you come over to my house?"

"Okay, but we don't really have anything to talk over." I hung up the phone and ran down the stairs.

On my way through the kitchen to go out the front door, I saw both my mom and grandma sitting down at the kitchen table. I told them I would be back soon because I had to go talk to Jenny real quick.

I got in my car and sped off. I turned the radio on and the song that was playing was, "Brown Eyed Girl." All the way there I was thinking, *I have to tell her the truth.*

The drive seemed longer than it really was, but I finally made it to Jenny's house. It was mainly back roads, so I was speeding a little. I looked toward Mary's sister's house as I stepped out of my car and walked toward Jenny's front door.

She quickly opened the front door and said, "Come in; let's go upstairs to my room and talk."

As we got to the top of the stairs, I said, "Wait a minute. Like I said on the phone, I just want to break up because I like another girl."

"Maybe we can work this out. Let's talk about it," she pleaded.

"There's nothing really to talk about. I just came over to tell you that I want to break up, and that's it."

She said sadly, "Okay."

As soon as I got home, I called up Mary and told her I wasn't going out with anyone anymore. She asked, "Why? What happened with you and Jenny?"

"I broke up with her, and you're the one I really want to be with."

"I told you I didn't want to cause any trouble between the two of you."

"You didn't tell me to break up with Jenny. That was my choice. Now how about it? Will you go out with me?"

"No, not right now. But since you say you and Jenny aren't going together right now, if you want, you can call me later."

I said, "Okay, I can do that. So what are you doing right now?"

"I have to go uptown with my sister, Julia, because we have to pick up a few things."

"Okay, we'll talk later then."

She said, "All right, bye."

I don't think what I did had anything to do with it, but shortly after that happened, Jenny's family moved a few miles away into a nice, two-story, light-blue-and-yellow house out in the country.

Mary and Jenny talked about what happened between the two of us. Mary told Jenny, "Johnny asked me if I would go out with him."

Jenny said, "If you want to go out with him, that's okay with me, and we can still be friends."

In the meantime, I had been calling Mary and telling her how nice I thought she always looked and how different she was from all the other girls I had known before her. I was trying everything that I knew to get her to be my girlfriend. I hadn't ever tried so hard or wanted a girl to go out with me so badly. I felt like, this time, it was for all the marbles. It seemed like an eternity, but in reality, it had only been three days. That was because normally when I had my eye on a girl and went after her, I got her to go out with me in under a day. If I wanted to go out with a certain girl and she knew about it, it was on like Donkey Kong. Now that's what I was used to. The Lord humbled me, while at the same time teaching me how to have patience and the importance of being persistent. I needed that.

All during those three days, of course, I was playing it like Mr. Cool and making it look like having to wait didn't really bother me.

After the three days were up, I called Mary to have what I thought was our usual daily talk, and she pleasantly surprised me. She said, "I had a talk with Jenny, and she told me that if I wanted to go out with you, it was okay with her. She wouldn't get angry, and we could still be friends."

So I asked her, "Will you go out with me?"

"If we were boyfriend and girlfriend, I could answer you," she said with a little, flirtatious chuckle.

With confidence, I asked, "Okay, Mary, will you be my girlfriend?" She said, "Yes." I could tell in her voice that she was happy.

I said, "All right! Where do you want to go?"

"I don't know where my mom will let me go."

I said, "I don't know what's playing at the movies, but if you want to go see a movie, I'll take you. Or if you would rather go take a walk in the park, that's cool with me too."

"I have to ask permission first."

"Yeah, that's cool."

"Hang on. Let me go ask."

Since it was a Saturday, I thought her mom would say it would be okay for her to go out with me for a little while. When she got back on the phone, she said, "My mom said we needed to get to know you a little better first."

"Well, I can come over right now if she wants."

"No, let's take it slow." She said that because she had talked with her mother and older sister; taking things slow was one piece of much advice they had given her on how to act when she had a boyfriend. She added, "My brother-in-law, Alex, is going to take Julia, my sister, and the children to the carnival tonight, and they invited me to go with them. We could see each other there if you're going to the carnival tonight."

I asked her, "What time will you be there?"

"Alex said we were going to leave from here at seven o'clock."

"Sounds good. I'll see you there."

We arrived at the carnival parking lot at the same time that night, and we had a great first date. It was one of only four before I asked her to marry me. Our dates all had to be on the weekends because that's the only time her folks would let her go out, which was cool with me. The way things happened for us, I believe to this day was all God orchestrated.

As we were talking one day on the telephone, I thought it was like all the other days. But I couldn't help noticing a little something different in her voice that I couldn't quite put my finger on. Then she let me have it and told me the news—she had to go back with her mother to Texas because work for them had ended. I've never claimed to be a brain like Einstein, but a blind person could see that was a situation that needed to be fixed. So I said, "You can't leave. What about us?"

She answered, "I don't know. All I know is my mom said we have to go back home."

Without missing a beat, I told her, "But I love you. What about if we were married?"

Surprised, she asked, "What?"

I could feel my heart, beating in my chest like a drum during a powwow meeting. With excitement in my voice I asked, "Will you marry me? You won't have to leave if you marry me, right?"

She sounded excited, surprised, and happy all at the same time when she said, "No, I wouldn't have to then."

I thought she felt the same as I did, but when she didn't answer me right away, I asked nervously again, "So will you marry me and stay?"

When she answered, "Yes, I will; I will marry you," I felt like I had just been told that $100 million was in the bank that I didn't know about and it was all mine.

As excited as I was, I was a little nervous too. Some emotions that I was not used to were running through me, but I was trying to keep my cool through all that. With a big smile on my face, I said, "You tell your mom and dad, and I'll tell mine."

She sounded a little nervous when she said, "Okay."

I was thinking, *I'm the luckiest young man in the world, and I'm only sixteen years old.* I said, "We'll talk later. I love you. Bye."

She said, "Okay. I love you. Bye."

The traditional Tex-Mex way of doing things when it came down to getting married was that both sides of the families would get to know each other first. Then the young man had someone, usually his mom and dad, go ask for the young lady's hand in marriage. After we told our parents, my mom and dad said they wanted me to bring Mary over, so they could get to know her. I asked my dad if I could use his van to go pick her up, and he said, "Yes, but take your little brother, Roman, with you."

I thought to myself, *Things are moving way to slow.*

The meeting between Mary and my family went fine, smooth as silk. When it was time to take Mary back home, I brought Roman with us again. But a little ways before we got to her house, I pulled over in a nice, little area where there was a park, so she and I could talk for a little bit.

I told her family, "We stopped at the little park that's on the way to your house so we could talk a little before I brought her home."

It seemed to me that no one in the family was too happy with what I had said. I tried to explain that we hadn't done anything wrong, and we weren't alone. My little brother, Roman, was with us all the time. They didn't really know me all that well, but I knew we had just talked about what was going to happen in our lives, and that was it. I told them, "My mom and dad are going to come over and ask for Mary's hand in marriage for me."

Mary's sister said, "We don't know what happened when you were at the park together."

That's when I said, "Well then, can I have Mary's hand in marriage?"

Mary's mom said, "Yes."

"That's great!" I said, beaming. "You all have a good night."

I didn't say anything to my little brother when I got back in the van, but when I got home. I explained to my mom dad and grandma everything that had happened. I told them, "You don't have to ask for Mary's hand in marriage for me anymore because I already did it, and her mom said yes."

My grandma said, "I knew you were going to do that. I thought to myself, *Johnny isn't going to wait.* I know how you are."

That was on the last Monday of the month. The next day, my mom and dad went over to Mary's sister's house and talked to Mary's mom, sister, and brother-in-law. They were acting on behalf of her dad, since he was back home in Texas.

After all was said and done, it was agreed; the wedding was set for that coming Saturday, September 3. So we had a lot to take care of and very little time to do it.

The day of the wedding finally came. The time for me making big decisions had started, and this was the first of many to come. I was married to a beautiful, young Latin lady, I had just turned sixteen, and I dropped out of high school after my sophomore year. For our honeymoon, I borrowed my dad's Custom Chevy van, and we went to the drive-in theater. I don't even remember what movies were playing at the time. That's not what was on my mind.

My new bride and I moved into my old room. It was the perfect size for the two of us.

Monday morning came around—a little too soon I thought—and it was time for work as a married man.

As I'd grown up in the fast lane, I learned and did some things that your normal teenager wouldn't do, while at the same time hoping, praying, and believing always in God's hand of protection on me and mine. I would always see my grandma going into her bedroom and I could hear her praying nice and loud. I know I was continually in her prayers, which was a blessing and a half for me and my new bride, but I had absolutely no idea of the wild journey that I was about to embark on in the not-so-distant future.

CHAPTER 5

A MISSOURI MULE HAD JUST KICKED ME

It was cold and you could tell it was getting to the end of fall. Our Nova hatchback got a crack in the exhaust by the muffler drum that kept coming back even after I found and patched it up. Each time, it would only hold together for a few days. Every kit I bought came with some cloth strips I had to dip into a solution I made after pouring a little water into a container that had some white powder in it. After mixing it up really well, I got the cloth strips and then dipped them into the mixture. I wrapped them around the cracked spot, and then turned the car engine on. After that spot got nice and hot, it would harden up, but after normal driving around, the strips that had hardened would break, and I could hear the difference every time it happened.

One day, I had to go into a nearby town by the name of Monuka. As I was driving into town, I saw a Ford dealership on my right side. I just so happened to glance over, and this shiny, red, short bed Ford truck with white pinstripes caught my eye. After finishing with the business I had in that little town, I drove home and told my dad all about the truck I saw. He told me it was still early enough if I wanted to go get a closer look at it.

I said, "Yeah, let's go, Dad."

I told Mary, "Dad is going with me to see a nice, little truck in the town of Monuka. We will be right back."

My dad told my mom, "I am going to take a look at a truck Johnny is telling me about." He turned looked at me and said, "Let's go in your car."

"Okay, Dad."

We drove into the Ford dealership, parked in front, and walked inside. One of the salesmen greeted us very nicely. "Can I help you gentlemen with anything?"

My dad said, "Yes, we want to look at that red truck you have in the front."

"Sure, let me just grab my coat and the keys." He had the keys in his hand and showed us the outside first. "We just got this in. It has a nice, candy apple red color with white pinstripes. It's like the old, classic, short bed, step side Fords." Then he unlocked the driver's side door and reached over and unlocked the passenger side door. "As you can see, it's an automatic. It has a nice, bright red color on the inside. You have plenty of room in here. You can see the gauges clearly. It has a nice, spacey glove box." He pushed the button, and it opened. As he handed my dad the keys, he asked, "Would you like to take it for a ride?"

My dad said, "It's for my boy."

"Oh, well I can't let you drive it because of your age," he told me. "But I can give you a ride in it and let you feel how it rides."

I said, "Okay."

There was snow on the ground. Maybe that was part of the reason why he didn't want to let me drive the truck by myself. I don't know. Anyway, he took me for a short ride away from town. He pulled into a place that sold butane gas that was close by and turned around.

Once we got back to the dealership and got out of the truck, he asked, "So, how did you like it?"

I said, "It was nice and smooth."

"Let's go into my office, and we can talk about it."

When we got into the dealership, my dad asked me in Spanish, "So how about it?"

I answered back in Spanish, "I liked it, Dad. It rides real nice."

"It's brand-new. It better ride real nice."

We both followed the man into his office. He said, "The boys took your car and checked it out. They said its well taken care of and you had worked on the motor. I can give you $2,200 for your car. The truck is a little over $6,000. Are you going to pay for it in cash? Or if you want to take it in payments for three years, your payments will be around $110 a month."

Again talking in Spanish, I asked my dad, "What do you think, Dad?" He turned the question around to me, "And what do you think? Will you be able to make the payments and pay the insurance?"

I told the man, "I don't know how much the insurance is going to be."

"I can look it up and tell you around how much it's going to be." He asked me my age.

I said, "Sixteen."

"And do you have any outstanding tickets?"

"No."

"How did you want to pay—every month, twice a year, or just once a year?"

"How much would it be if I wanted to pay twice a year?"

He looked it up, wrote a figure down on a piece of paper, and slid it over to me.

I looked at it and showed it to my dad. I told him in Spanish, "That looks pretty good. What do you think?"

My dad asked me again, "With what you make at the nursery, are you going to be able to pay for everything that needs to get paid?"

I thought for a couple seconds, and I answered him, "Yes."

"Well, tell the man you want the truck."

I looked at the man and said, "Sir, I'll take the truck."

"Okay great. Let me get the paperwork. I have a few questions for you."

After all the i's were dotted and the t's were crossed, we went home in a brand spanking new, short bed, step-side Ford F-150. This was my first new vehicle that was all my own. Well actually, it was mine and Mary's.

When we got home, I was all excited. I asked everyone inside if they wanted to check out the super nice-looking, new truck I had bought. But everybody said it was too cold. They would just wait till the morning when the sun was up.

I was new at this marriage business. I had to get used to it—I couldn't say with patience because I had very little of that, but thank God, with time.

It seemed like once I got that little red truck, *man*, did the devil ever work overtime on me. Let me be the one to tell you! First, I believe because the truck was new, the shape, and the candy apple red color, not to mention the young man behind the wheel was in pretty good physical shape, and not bad looking I heard, and yes, heads were turning. That young man was me, and yes, my head began to get enlarged, as I was meeting new people and they weren't the kind of people who went to church on Sundays.

One big temptation started with a magazine. It was a Wednesday after work, and the day thus far had been like any other regular day. After showering and eating, I told my wife and grandma, as I was heading out the door, "I'm going to the little convenience store in Pleasant Park. I'll be back later."

They both said, "Okay." My grandma added in Spanish, like usual, "God bless you my son."

I drove my truck right next to the gas pumps and filled it up. I walked inside the little store, said hi to the young lady running the cash register, turned to the right, and walked to the shelf that held the comic books and a variety of magazines, like I usually did. Except this time, I was about to make a choice that was going to affect my whole life from then on. I looked through a few comic books, some custom van magazines, and some that had to do with guns. I can't really remember exactly what kind of magazine I was looking in at the time, but I'll never forget the moment when I saw it, somewhere in the middle of all the little advertisements—out of the corner of my eye, I saw a small advertisement that said something like, "Own your very own book on witchcraft." You know what they say about curiosity and the cat. When I saw that, the first thing that came to mind was, *You can't buy a for real, true book on witchcraft in one of these normal magazines, especially from a regular convenience store.* I will have to admit, I hadn't ever seen anything like that before, and I haven't ever run across anything like that again. But it did get my curiosity going long enough to buy that magazine and take it home.

Once I had the magazine home, I reread the ad a couple of times again, but slower. I still had my doubts. It just seemed that you wouldn't be able to get a book on the occult or real, live witchcraft so easily. But the ad said that, once I got the book, I would have thirty days to check it out, and if for any reason I didn't like it, all I would have to do is return it and I wouldn't have to pay a dime. It seemed like a win-win situation to me. I cut the little piece of advertisement out, filled everything out that was needed, and mailed it off.

To my surprise, within a week's time, I received in the mail something that looked about the size of a book, discretely wrapped in a cardboard cover with an easy peel-off tab. I peeled off the tab, opened up the package, and saw a book inside. Turning the package upside down, I slid the book out; it had a nice, smooth, black cover with a dirty yellow-colored bold title that read, *Witchcraft Power.* I was surprised, first, because of the short amount of time it had taken to get a response and, second, because I was able to get it—a real book on the occult—through the mail.

I took the book into our bedroom to look it over and to tell Mary that it had already came in.

She said, with a little bit of disbelief in her voice, "Let me see."

The book instructed me to pick a special room where only witchcraft would be done there. Because we were living at my mom and dad's house, I knew I wouldn't be able to prepare a room the way the book Instructed. For starters, I would have to wash the entire room from top to bottom with water that had sea salt mixed in with it, (so many teaspoons of sea salt for each gallon of water). Then I would have to paint the entire room, either off white or black. It had to have some big dark curtains, because the room was supposed to be as dark as possible when performing witchcraft in there. I would also need to measure from my belly button to the floor (without any shoes or socks of course). I would use that length to make a circle where I would be protected from any negative spirits. I could just picture myself sitting in an Indian position with my legs crossed, or on my knees. I could have a little table in the circle with me, but it couldn't have any metal in it. I could just imagine if I was to tell my grandma I needed a room to perform witchcraft in. She would have a royal fit if she had any kind of an idea I was entertaining the thought of preparing a room for that reason. But I found it interesting, so I decided to pay for the book and keep it for the day we got our own place. That way, I could fix up a room. It would be a specially picked room, where I could practice witchcraft, and I could do a lot of meditation to prepare myself.

After I'd sent in the payment for the first book and the thirty days to check it out had expired, to my surprise, I got another book dealing with the occult in the mail. The same company from whom I'd purchased the first book gave me the same thirty days to check it out. If for any reason I didn't like it, I could send it back and, once again, not have to pay a dime.

Altogether, I ended up getting a small collection of about thirteen books, all on the occult. Of all the books the publisher sent me, I only ended up returning one book because I didn't feel it was on the same level as any of the other books.

I hadn't ever read a book from cover to cover before; I never was a reader. But I did read through all of the books that came in the mail, always looking for something that would make me different but, at the same time, the same as everybody else. I just wanted it to look as if I was a regular person off the street who seemed to have luck following me all the time. That was when I believed in luck.

I would still always pray at night and read my Bible, but the devil is sly. I believe the devil provided me the perfect rationalization; yes, they're about magic, I reasoned, but at least it's not black magic. And it would be okay for me to dabble in it, as long as I didn't have to sell my soul or hurt anybody. I hadn't read in any of the books about any blood sacrifices that needed to be made. I thought, *These books are cool. They don't show you how to hurt other people, and if what they say is really true I will have the power to make things happen all around me.* I would be in control.

I hadn't tried anything that was in any of the books yet. My thinking was that simply owning the collection of books on the occult was cool. I was still skeptical. I thought, *How in the world can a person make things happen in his or her life just by simply saying some words?* I do remember reading that what I chose to make happen for other people would come back to me, and it does say in the Bible, " Do not be deceived, God is not mocked; for whatever a man sows, that he will also reap" (Galatians 6:7 NKGV).

I finally decided on a book I thought was perfect for me. It didn't say anything about needing a special room. I thought, *Let me give it a try.*

I hadn't ever really been taught to be scared of anything. However, my parents had told me to stay away from certain people who were known to be involved with drugs and things like that. The way I like to put it is, "Don't mess around with the underground." But did I listen?

Not even for the life of me.

The name of the book I chose was something like, *The Magic Power in You.* In the introduction, it said, "You can have love always looking for you, money chasing you down, power over anyone, and protection against all evil." The book also incorporated words from the Bible. It said things like, "You do not have because you do not ask," and explained that the word *amen* and the phrase *as I will, so will it be* were synonymous. While *amen* is usually used at the end of a prayer, when talking to Almighty God, the words *as I will, so will it be* are often used when performing magic spells. (That is like comparing apples and oranges.) I had heard and knew a lot of words that were in the Bible, thanks to my grandma, so I thought, *For sure this book can't be all that bad, if it has words from the Bible.*

The one thing I didn't agree with was the book's claim that I had to only ask the gods that represented whatever it was I wanted or, in other words, pray to other gods. That was where the curveball came in. I knew better, but my curiosity was still saying, *What if this really works?*

So I tried it. I did everything how the book said to do it. And to my surprise, every single thing I asked for, I got.

Right after I asked for money, a young man I didn't even know about came up from our home town of Las Palomas and got a job at the same nursery were I worked. As we talked during the time we were at work, I found out that we were related. We were around the same age and had a few things in common. To mention just a couple, we were both married and liked a lot of the same things, one being to smoke marijuana. I thought, *Since he came and got a job at the nursery, he knows he needs to work in order to have money for his bills. So he's not just a freeloader trying to take advantage of other people's kindness.*

After work he asked me, "Can you go pick me up at my Aunt Consuelo's house where my wife and I are staying, so we can hang out together?"

I told him, "I haven't ever been there before, but if you tell me how to get there, I'll see you there."

After he gave me the directions, I went home like usual, took a shower, and ate. I told my wife, "I met this guy at work today and found out we're cousins, and I'm going to pick him up from where he's staying in Kewanee at his aunt's house."

When I got to the house, I honked the horn a couple of times, and he came out right away. When he got in the truck, I asked him, "Where do you want to go?"

He said, "I don't know. Is there a bar where the guys from the nursery usually hang around at?"

"Yeah, at a bar called The Lucky Star. The owner's name is Lucinda."

"Well, let's go check out Lucinda."

On the way there, he asked me, "Do you have any mota already twisted up with you, bro?

I knew what he meant when he asked that. I hadn't ever heard marijuana called that before, but I said, "Yeah, some Colombian Gold. Check out the baggie in the glove box."

He opened the glove box and took a joint I had already twisted up from the baggie; I had another joint in there with some shake and rolling papers for the road. For those of you who aren't familiar with the word *shake*, in drug lingo, that simply means what falls off the marijuana buds. I always liked to be prepared in case I felt like firing one up, which was about all the time. Colombian Gold, to me, was the best I had ever known. It had a nice yellow-gold color, accompanied by a sweet taste. Bottom line, it was just the best around town

I told him, "I know the people who sell it, so whenever I run out, I always know where to go to get more."

He told me, "It's not bad, but I've had better. How long does the buzz last?"

"Twenty minutes to half an hour, depending on what you're doing at the time."

We smoked that one all up, and he asked, "Can we smoke the other one you have in there?"

"Yeah, whip it out, bro."

By the time we finished the second one, we were outside of Lucinda's place. This was on a Wednesday, and the sun hadn't even gone all the way down yet. But I took him there anyway, so he couldn't say he hadn't ever been at Lucinda's.

He said, "It looks pretty dead in here, bro."

I told him, "Starting on Fridays is when she really pulls the crowds in, and then it's booming."

I introduced him to Lucinda, and we had a few drinks there with her.

After about a half hour passed, only a couple of people had stopped by. So I told him, "Let's get out of here. We can stop by some other day." I took him home and told him, "I'll see you tomorrow at work."

"Okay, bro."

He worked at the nursery a couple more weeks, and then he said, "I have to go back home to Las Palomas because my dad is sick." So his supervisors at the nursery told him at work it would be okay; he could go see about his dad.

He was only gone for a week, and then he was back at work. He told me, "I brought something that I want to show you after work." I noticed that his eyes looked all bloodshot, but I thought, *Maybe he has allergies.*

I said, "Okay." As I was adjusting my hat, I was trying to imagine what it might be.

He motioned for me to wait and said, "So we don't have to stay at my aunt's house anymore, my dad bought us a little house that's close to her house."

I told him, "Just tell me how to get there, and I'll see you there after work."

As he was walking slowly toward the time clock to punch in, he said, "It's just a block away from my aunt's house. You take the same road as when you're going to her house, but when you get to the end of the block, instead of turning to the right, you just turn left. My house is the one on the corner."

I had already punched my time card and was walking speedily toward the big barn, where the tractor I drove was. "Okay, that sounds pretty easy," I said. "I'll see you there after work."

When five o'clock finally rolled around and it was time to go home, after doing everything I usually did after work, I told my wife, "Let's go visit my cousin Arthur and Linda at their new house."

She said, "Okay. I didn't even know they were back yet, and I haven't seen Linda for a while."

I followed his directions and parked the truck on the side of the road. We walked over to the front door and didn't even get to knock before Linda answered the door and said, "Come on in. Arthur is in the kitchen."

He said, "Hey, come in, bro. I just finished eating." I asked him, "How was it?"

"I didn't like it," he said as he was wiping his mouth.

His wife said, "Yeah right. That's why you ate everything, including some of the flowers off the bottom of the plate."

As we all laughed, he was getting up from the table and going into the living room. He waved us toward the living room and said, "Come in here. Sit down and make yourselves comfortable." He told his wife, "Get me the garbage bag from the closet."

She went in their bedroom and brought out a large, black garbage bag and gave it to him.

As he was looking at me he said, "Come here and look at this." He opened the mouth of the bag, and inside, I saw a few bundles in the shape of extra-large footballs, with a slice in one of them. He pulled out a small marijuana bud from the slice and squeezed it between his pointing finger and thumb. When he opened his fingers apart, the bud stuck to his thumb. He asked me to smell it.

I said, "That stuff is still green. It even looks and smells green." I asked him, "Did you get it from some ditch or what?"

"You're crazy. This is high-grade stuff. Mexican red hair sinsemilla is the best there is."

Well, I hadn't ever seen or heard of Sinsemilla before. The only kind of marijuana from Mexico I had ever heard of or dealt with was real low-grade stuff. It smelled bad, tasted bad, and would probably give you a headache. I likened it to ditch weed.

I was very badly mistaken in this case, and I would very soon find out that looks can be deceiving—especially if you don't know what you're looking at or what you're looking for. He said, "My telephone is hooked up, so if you have some friends who you know are good people and you can trust them, call and tell them to get some money together."

I told him, "Okay, let me make a phone call."

I dialed to my friend Mack's house and said, "Hey, Mack, what are you doing? Are you busy?"

"No, Johnny, what's up?"

"A cousin of mine just came up from Texas and brought a few pounds of Mexican Sinsemilla. Do you have a few good guys you can call, and tell them to wait for us there at your house? In about half an hour, we'll be there to show them some real good, fresh stuff."

He said, "Okay, come on over."

"We'll be there after a little bit." I told Arthur, "Now you better not make me look bad. We're going to meet a few guys over at my friend Mack's house. He's going to call a few of the guys he knows."

"That sounds cool, bro. Let's go."

He told his wife Linda, "We'll be back later." I told Mary, "Yeah, we won't be long."

He grabbed the bag and closed it up and then put it into a large brown paper bag. We both got into the truck, and we were headed toward Mack's House. On the way, Arthur quickly rolled one up and lit it, took a couple of hits, and passed it to me. I was about to experience something I hadn't ever experienced before—not even in my wildest dreams. The weed still smelled kind of green to me. So when I took the joint, I inhaled it deeply. It tasted a little minty, and I held the hit in for a few seconds. We were going over a bridge as I blew it out and said, "I don't feel anything."

I took another deep hit and held it; all of a sudden, *BAM!* I felt like a Missouri mule had just kicked me in the back of the head, without a hint of a warning. That's one of the best ways to describe the very first time I smoked Mexican red hair sinsemilla.

We had just started rolling down the road for a little ways, and I said to my cousin, "Man, bro, that's some gooood stuff. I haven't ever checked anything like this out before. I know we won't have a hard time getting rid of this."

We didn't even finish the whole joint; I just put it in the ashtray and left it there. I was driving, so I'm glad I left that bad boy in there by itself. When we finally pulled into Mack's driveway, I told Arthur, "Grab the stuff and let's go show them some true Mexican Sinsemilla."

We both walked to his front door. I knocked.

Mack said, "Come on in, Johnny."

"Hey, Mack, why don't you feast your eyes on this?" I looked at Arthur, and said, "Roll a couple up and let these guys really check it out."

Including Mack, a total of seven guys had gathered. So Arthur rolled some nice, healthy-sized joints; that way, everybody could get the true feeling from it. I wanted the guys to get kicked by the same Missouri mule.

After everybody got a chance to look it over, smell it, and take a couple of hits off one of those miniature stogies, everybody was happy, and the guys were asking how much for a pound.

I asked them, "Have any of you ever seen or smoked any Mexican red hair sinsemilla before?"

Some of them said, "Yeah, but not around here."

"And what was the going price for it at that time?"

I heard from around eleven to twelve hundred dollars a pound. So I told them, "This stuff has got to go fast, so nine hundred dollars will get you a pound."

The closest guy to me said, "I want a pound."

Okay, Mack, do you have a scale and some baggies?"

He said, "All I have is this little handheld scale."

"That will do for right now."

"I don't have any baggies. But we could weigh this brown paper bag by itself and then start putting some weed in it until we get the weight you want."

That day, I told the guys that, whoever didn't take a pound for nine hundred could have half a pound for five hundred. When it was all done and over with, everybody was happy; and all five pounds went at that precise moment. My cousin had a pocketful of money, and all the other guys had the best weed in town. On Monday, Arthur asked my dad if he could let the owners know at the nursery that he was needed back home and to tell them thanks for the job.

About two weeks later, I had just gotten home from work and went up to our room; the phone rang, so I answered it. The man's voice on the other end of the line asked in Spanish, "Is this Johnny?"

"Yes it is," I said.

"My name is Hando," the man said, his voice deep and raspy. "Arthur told me about you. He said you're a good man."

"Yeah, he's my cousin." My reservations about the unknown caller were gone as soon as he mentioned Arthur.

"I'm at Lucinda's right now," Hando continued, his tone businesslike but pleasant. "If you want to stop by and talk, I'll buy you a drink."

"Sure," I agreed, curious now. "I'll see you in a few minutes."

When I got to Lucinda's, not many cars were in the parking lot, even though it was a Friday. But it was still kind of early, and anyway, I hadn't gone there to party and get drunk. When I walked in, I noticed a man with a cowboy hat who I hadn't ever seen before. I felt good vibes coming from him. Meeting a man who Arthur had recommended me to seemed kind of exciting to me. I greeted Lucinda, sat on a barstool right next to the man in the cowboy hat, and started talking with him as if we had known each other from before.

He asked me, "What do you want to drink?"

As Lucinda was walking over toward us, I told her, "Get me the usual, a Jack and Coke."

"Is it always this quiet here?" he asked, looking at me without making it obvious that he had already scoped out the whole bar.

"It's still early," I said, "and a lot more people should be arriving after a few hours to start the night off."

After looking at me all nonchalant, he said, "Well in that case, let's go out to my truck so I can show you something."

After we finished our drinks, we went outside and headed over toward his truck, which was parked in front and over to the left side of the bar.

Before we got into his truck, he opened his driver's side door, leaned the back part of his seat forward, and reached back there. He took a large, black garbage bag from the back. After he fixed the seat, he brought it to the front with us. He opened the bag, stuck his hand in, and took out a pinch of something that looked green. Once I got a better look, I could see it was a marijuana bud. It was green-looking with some yellow in it and a lot of red hairs running from top to bottom. He broke it apart with his fingers and, as he brought it close to his nose, he said, "Smell it. It's real fresh and potent."

"Yes, I can tell."

"Look it over. If you're interested, I can help you out by letting you keep it. After you sell it, I'll check back with you in about three weeks."

I hadn't ever really done "the selling of drugs thing" before, but it sounded kind of interesting to me. So I agreed. "Okay," I told him, "but I parked my truck on the other side of the bar."

"I'll drive you over there, so you don't have to carry this in the open."

That was the start of me becoming a professional drug dealer. I got to see high-grade marijuana of all different colors and shapes that came to me in bundles in a variety of sizes and shapes. Some packages looked like the bases from a baseball game, while others looked like oversized footballs. I even got to see something that looked like a bale of hay that was composed entirely of compacted, high-grade marijuana.

In order to learn more about different kinds of marijuana, I started looking at and buying magazines that talked about and showed close up pictures of some real nice-looking buds. Several times, to my surprise, I even saw some pictures of some marijuana buds that looked exactly like the stuff that was brought to me.

On a number of occasions, I got to see money and things exchanged from one person to another, all in the name of drugs. I started to notice people wanting to hang around me more because they knew I usually had the best herb around. I was always smoking it without measure, or I didn't hold back on the left-handed cigarettes. The way I always thought was, *There's plenty more where that came from.*

Since I was a little boy I had always been taught to share, especially if I had plenty. The way I always saw it was, *Since I got to cop a good buzz and get mellowed out, I wanted everybody to have the same opportunity and get a marijuana experience they would want again and again, at a below-average price.*

About a month and a half after I first met with Hando, he got his money for the merchandise he had left with me. My cut was whatever I could get above seven hundred fifty dollars a pound and as much high-grade marijuana as I wanted to smoke—plus whatever extras came with it (like all the recognition that came from having the best herb around, for the lowest price available).

Eventually, I got to meet new people I heard of who sold marijuana. But when I let them try a left-handed cigarette of the stuff that I had for sale, I would give them the same opportunity that had been given to me; in other words, I was willing to front to them. I found out that just because I knew the people that didn't necessarily mean I knew the people's ways of doing business. When I first got started in this business, I thought everybody paid their debts or that, if someone was decent enough to believe in you and let you have something of value without making you pay for it first, then after you sold that thing of value, you would want to pay for it, without a hassle. It didn't take me long to find out, unfortunately, that isn't always the case.

Some people I dealt with I had known for a number of years. A lot of them were the same people I had the hardest time with when it came to getting my money. It took me a few years to see, but I finally realized there were some people who I couldn't trust as far as I could throw them. I didn't feel I should have to go around chasing after them, telling them over and over I wanted my money. That seemed like too much of a hassle to me. I didn't have time for those kinds of childish games.

After a few years of trial and error, during which I disconnected myself from the people I couldn't trust and got closer with the good, trustworthy people, for a while, it was smooth sailing. The group of people who were known to deal with drugs down in the valley, from South Texas, talked about me in a good way. People involved in that business talked to each other about their experiences, identifying the good, trustworthy people, as well as the bad people—those who would give them a hard time when it came to getting their money or their merchandise back. Different people from the group started calling me, telling me they had heard good things about me and how they knew Hando and Arthur. The conversation always ended up with them asking me, "Do you want to meet somewhere so I can show you something?"

After I met with them and they showed me the merchandise they had, most of them would leave me with these famous last words: "I can help you out; I'll leave this with you right now and check back with you after a few weeks."

What they left behind was in my possession. I was responsible for the stuff. I was selling it. And in the end, I would give them their money. Now who was really helping who out? "You can fool some of the people some of the time, but you can't fool all the people all the time."

One of the times Hando called me. At this point, we were already established associates. He asked me, "Are you going to be home?"

I answered, "Yes."

"I'm on the road right now, and I'll be by your house after the sun goes down," he told me.

"Sounds good," I said. "I'll be watching for you."

When nighttime came around, I heard a vehicle pulling into my mom and dad's driveway. From our bedroom window, I could see it was

Hando's truck. So I hurried down the stairs and out the door. He parked a little distance away from the house. Before I got to where he was, I could see he was out of his truck and doing something underneath it. At first I thought, *Maybe something's wrong with his truck.*

But after he came out, he had the spare tire with him. He tossed it in the back of the truck. I climbed back there and asked him, "What do you have there?"

"This is how I crossed the checkpoint with the mota," he explained. "It's in the spare tire, and then it gets bolted on underneath."

That was a pretty reliable way of crossing the checkpoint and not getting caught with a load of guaranteed jail time, so we did it that way a few more times.

He said, "We have to get all the bundles out that are in the tire. Do you have a big knife so we can cut it open? We also need a large garbage bag. Do you have one?"

I said, "I think so. Let me go see."

I jumped off the truck and ran into the kitchen, where I looked around where the garbage bags should be. And, *yes!* I found one. I grabbed the biggest kitchen knife I saw and ran back to the truck. Hando had a decent-sized pocketknife with him, so he was able to get one bundle out from the tire by the time I got back. He straightened it up and shook it to see where he could hear the rest. "I can hear something on the left side."

I helped him, and we got the last four out. We put all five bundles in the garbage bag. I closed it up and jumped with it on the ground. He jumped out of the back and got in front. I said, "I will see you later."

He said, "Yeah," as he started to drive away.

Without thinking about how I was going to get the bag with all the bundles into our room, I walked fast toward one side of our house by the kitchen window. I swung the bag over my head and threw it onto the part of the roof that was right in front of our bedroom window. I went inside and put the kitchen knife in the sink, ran upstairs, closed our door, locked it, went over to the window, and unlocked the screen. I grabbed the garbage bag with the bundles and pulled it in the room. That was one of the first times Hando and I had one of those short, but intense moments. And it wouldn't be the last time either. On that particular evening, we at least had the cover of night. But day or night, because I had not ever really been taught to be afraid of anything that looked negative in life, the callous that had grown over time took advantage of me. So fear was never an option.

CHAPTER 6

METALLIC BLUE RENEGADE CJ-5 JEEP TIME

It started out looking like any other Saturday morning. After getting up and doing what I normally did when I didn't have to go to work on a Saturday, I decided to go for a cruise in my pickup truck. Keep in mind, I didn't act, think, or speak like your average seventeen-year-old. I've heard, "An idle mind is the devil's playground," which was especially true for me if I didn't have to go to work. I will admit, my mind was pretty mellowed out or, like I like to put it, I was just chillin' like a villain.

After driving around for a while, I ended up at The Lucky Star. The men from the nursery who were the most dedicated to Lucinda's place would even go right after work. They wouldn't even bother to eat or take a shower. Can you imagine the smell, especially after a hot summer day after work? Lucinda didn't mind that, as long as they left their money there with her. Most of the other men, including myself, would only go on the weekends, after eating and taking a good shower.

On one particular Saturday, my uncle Cisco—my dad's only brother who lived about thirty miles away in another little town southeast of us—had decided to stop and visit Lucinda. He had been there before many times. One of the main reasons he liked going there was the company. Most of the time, especially on the weekends, a number of the regulars were the crazy, wild, and rowdy type of men and women. Usually after midnight, or after everyone had a few drinks in them, whichever came first, that's when the crazy, wild rowdiness would start manifesting in most of the people.

On this certain night, my uncle had gotten a head start on me. At about twelve thirty that night, my uncle was feeling pretty good. I told him, "Everybody seems to be nice and mellowed out. Do you want to go for a ride with me in my truck so I can smoke one?"

My uncle knew I didn't ever smoke cigarettes, but he still said, "Sure."

After we got outside, he said, "Let's take my truck instead." It was a nice, brand spanking new red Ford Bronco with a white top. Plus it was a four-wheel drive to boot. As he handed me his keys, he asked me, "Do you want to drive?"

I hadn't ever driven a Bronco before. But the way my dad taught me is, as long as you know where the brakes, gas, and clutch are and how many gears it has, you're okay. His truck was an automatic, so that was even better. I said, "Sure I'll drive."

After unlocking my door, I got in and unlocked his door. He got in; I turned the truck on and put it in reverse. We drove out of the parking lot and headed south. I immediately took out the only left-handed cigarette I had with me, lit it up, and offered him some. I thought that would be the polite thing to do. But he said, "No thanks."

After driving for a few minutes, I turned to the right on the second side road coming from the bar. It was a gravel road, but it was a road. After smoking my left-handed cigarette all up, I threw the roach out the window for safety reasons. (For those of you not familiar with the term *roach*, in the drug lingo, that simply means what's left over after smoking a marijuana cigarette). That way, if the police were to stop and search us, or look in the ashtray, they wouldn't find anything. I told my uncle, "I haven't ever driven a four-wheel drive truck before. Can I try yours in four-wheel drive?"

He said, "Sure."

"What do I have to do first?" I asked.

"Go outside and twist the red locks in the middle of the two front tires to the right so it can pull with the front tires too."

I did and got back in the truck.

Then he said, "Now move that little shifter on the floorboard into four high."

So I did that. It was early springtime. All the snow out in the fields had melted. It looked a little wet, sloppy, and muddy. So it was perfect for four wheeling and making mud fly all over the place. A little ways under the mud, the ground was still frozen. I was used to riding my dirt bike and making what is called a rooster tail with my back tire by making mud fly backward high up in the air. I really liked that. That's what I called having fun. But to be able to make mud fly with all four tires at the same time, now that's what I was talking about.

After shifting into drive, I slowly drove toward the right, into a cornfield that had been harvested in the previous fall season. All of a sudden, I stepped on the gas pedal and sharply turned the steering wheel toward the left. I made a donut twice in the same spot and then, turning the steering wheel sharply and suddenly to the right, made another double donut. Since the two were connected, the marking in the field looked like a figure eight. Then I eased my foot off the gas pedal and slowly drove back onto the gravel road.

After my uncle straightened up a little in his seat he said, "I'll take it from here. I was feeling a little drunk, but I'm completely sober now."

We both laughed.

After I moved the little shifter on the floorboard back to neutral, I opened my door and got out. As I was going by the front tire on my side, I unlocked that wheel. I kept on going around the front end of the truck, and when I reached the other side, I unlocked that wheel also.

After we switched places, my uncle drove both of us back to The Lucky Star. On the way there, he said, "I'm going home after I drop you off."

I said, "Yeah, me too."

So when he pulled into the parking lot, after we'd said our good-byes, I got out and went to my truck. After having so much fun in my uncle's four-wheel drive Bronco, I just had to have some kind of a four-wheel drive vehicle.

After about four months had passed, it just so happened—or at least that's what I thought at the moment—that I was driving by a motorcycle shop that also sold used cars, and right in front was a really nice-looking, metallic blue Jeep. I pulled over to check it out a little closer. I hadn't ever seen a Jeep up close before, so I went around looking at it from all sides. While I was glancing in through the windows, I noticed that it was a stick shift. I hadn't ever owned a vehicle with a stick shift in it before, so I was impressed with what I saw. I had plenty of practice driving a few motorcycles that my dad had bought for me when I was younger. The last two were from the same motorcycle shop. I also had practice driving the nursery's tractors, which were all stick shift. Most of the vehicles at work had manual transmissions, so I had plenty of practice driving and shifting gears.

A salesman from the dealership came out and asked me, "How are you doing today?"

I answered, "Great!"

"My name is Steve," he said. "Can I help you with anything?"

"Yeah, I like the way this Jeep looks."

He did his job and started off by telling me how it was a beauty with a new ragtop. He also explained it was a four on the floor, powered by a strong V-6 engine, and good on gas. I could see that it had a lift kit and four nice, big, fat knobby tires. When I opened the driver's-side door, I could also see that it had new carpeting on the floor. I liked how the gauges looked nice, big, and easy to read. I noticed that it didn't have a backseat. One thing I really liked about the Jeep was that it had bucket seats.

Everything sounded and looked really nice to me, except for the V-6 engine part. I hadn't ever owned a vehicle with a V-6 engine in it before. But then again, I hadn't ever owned a 4x4 either.

After Steve was done showing me the Jeep, I was sold on it right away. Later, I found out that looks can be deceiving. I usually asked my dad for his opinion, especially when it came to making big choices. But this time, I didn't. That was a big mistake on my part.

I was eighteen years old at the time, and the truck was in my name. So I was able to make an even trade—my truck for the Jeep. Later on, it dawned on me that I'd bought the truck new from a dealership, while the Jeep, though it had a nice paint job on the outside, was used, and the trade may not have been in my favor. But I wanted a 4x4, and blue was my favorite color. Metallic blue; now that really caught my eye. The stick shift had a solid, aluminum handgrip that fit in my hand just perfectly.

Later on, I would know the meaning of, "Not all that glitters is gold." Bottom line, I traded my truck in for the Jeep, without even talking it over with my wife or asking my dad's opinion.

When I brought the Jeep home, my mom and dad and the rest of the family were in the dining room. Some of them had looked through the window to see who was driving in.

I told everybody, "Hey, you guys, it's me. Come outside so you can get a better look at the Jeep I just got." I wanted everyone to see the great deal I'd just made.

My wife and everyone else came out to see it.

"I'll be able to climb up a telephone pole with this," I told them.

My brother-in-law said, "You will be able to climb the sandhills of Wawpecong out east easily."

"Let's go check them out," I suggested. "Mary, do you want to go with us?" I asked my wife.

"No thanks," she said. "I'll pass."

I told them, "I don't even know how to get out there; I've never been there before."

But George, my brother-in-law, said, "I have. I know how to get there."

"All right!" I said. Then I asked, "Hey, Falcon, are you, George, and Paula ready to climb some hills?"

My wife and I had a blue beanbag chair upstairs in our room. "I'll be right back," I said. I ran inside the house and up the stairs to our room. Once there, I grabbed the beanbag chair off the floor and brought it down.

"Excuse me," I said to everyone still gathered around the Jeep. "This will fit just right in the back." After I threw the beanbag chair into the back, I said, "Okay, now we're ready to roll."

Then we all climbed into the Jeep and headed out east.

After driving about fifteen minutes, we came to a crossroad. My brother-in-law said, "Drive across this road and onto the dirt road and keep on going until you get to a road made completely of sand."

We finally got to the road made completely of sand. I looked straight ahead, to the right, and to the left. It was like driving into another world. As far as I could see there was sand, trees, and trails. After I turned to the right and drove for about a quarter of a mile, I saw the tallest sandhill I had ever seen in my life. A few trees stood on top, and a few lined the bottom of the hill. So I drove slowly around the front of the giant sandhill to check it out and picked the last trail going up the hill. I didn't even bother to turn the Jeep off. I just put it in neutral, got out, and locked both of the front hubs.

Then I climbed back inside the Jeep and stepped on the clutch. I shifted the little shifter on the floor into four low, and then I shifted into first gear. I eased off the clutch and slowly started driving. It felt and sounded like an army tank. I shifted it into second gear and then into third, which felt and sounded much better. I was more or less experimenting. The Jeep felt so powerful in my hands. I wasn't accustomed to owning something with so much power. I told everybody to hang on as I lined up with the trail going up the hill.

I hadn't ever tried this before, so when I came to a spot with a dip about halfway up the hill, I didn't know what to do. The Jeep started to sound like it was about to turn off on me. I stepped on the clutch and shifted into first gear and then popped the clutch out as I punched the gas pedal down. But to my surprise, all four tires started digging into the hill. I'd thought that, because it was a Jeep and because of the way the motor sounded, getting stuck in the middle of a sandhill would be impossible. But that was exactly what happened. I stepped on the clutch and shifted into reverse as I quickly popped the clutch out and punched the gas pedal down again. The Jeep started moving back, but since the front tires were slightly turned to the right, the back end started turning to the right. I quickly stepped on the clutch again and shifted into first, popped the clutch out, and punched the gas pedal down. The Jeep went forward for about a foot and a little deeper into the hill. I shifted back into reverse while turning the front wheels to the right even more. I popped the clutch out while giving it gas, and the Jeep moved backward about a foot once again. I wanted to keep rocking it back and forth.

We ended up sideways in the middle of a very tall hill, looking down at the place where we'd first started. In short, I just turned it all the way around right in the middle of the sandhill and drove it back down, front end first. Now that was something I hadn't ever heard of or seen, not even on TV. I thought, *That was cool.* To me, that was fun.

I also remember that, during that time in my life, I was buzzed about 97 percent of the time (maybe even more).

After we safely got down the hill, I said, "We'd better go home now. I'll be back another day."

After a few weeks of driving around in the Jeep, I got comfortable sitting behind the steering wheel of any 4x4. I like to take things to the extreme, so for me it was Renegade CJ-5 time! I thought, *It's time to fly like an eagle.*

I had no idea that thought was a prophecy. On one special Saturday, a day that looked really nice, in part because it had stated raining a little and we didn't have to work, I needed to go get some money that this guy owed me, from what I like to call my second job. He was a client—or in other words, a dealer of—mine, and he lived a couple of towns away.

"I'll be back later," I told my wife as I was walking toward the door of our room. "I have to go see a man about a dog; he lives in Wilsonville."

She didn't know exactly what I meant by that, but she still answered, "Okay, I'll see you later."

I went downstairs and saw my grandma as I passed through the kitchen. I said in Spanish, "Hi, grandma, I have to go uptown. I'll be back later."

She answered me back in Spanish, "Okay. Be careful, and God bless you my son."

I got in my Jeep and headed toward Wilsonville. I turned the radio on; what was playing was The Joker and took one of my left-handed cigarettes out of the left front pocket of my favorite blue jean jacket. I noticed that the roads looked shiny and everything had gotten a nice, light sprinkle of rain.

I didn't exactly remember at that time (but I would later) that just after a light rain—because the gas and oil and whatever other liquids may have fallen on the road get all mixed up—is when the roads are the slipperiest. That's when it's the easiest for any vehicle's tires to slide around. I like taking back roads just about anywhere I go. So I took the back way to my friend's house.

On the way there, I slowed down at the first stop sign and looked to the left and then to the right as I slowly continued turning right. On my way to the stoplight I saw that the arrow on the stoplight for me to turn left was green, so I shifted once, twice, three times. I wasn't speeding, but I was moving too fast to slam my brakes on and stop all of a sudden. As the arrow on the stoplight had just turned yellow for me, I wasn't quite in the middle of the intersection, but I had already started going that way. A car opposite me was waiting, and his light was about to turn green. As I was making the turn, the momentum and the weight of the Jeep caused it to start sliding sideways. When the Jeep finally caught, my two right-side tires stayed on the road while my two left-side tires went up in the air; I was still midturn. When I got to the straightaway, my two left-side tires came back down on the road. So in short, I made the turn with only my two right-side tires touching the road. The results couldn't have been better if the maneuver had been choreographed and I was a professional stunt driver, which I wasn't. The only two viewers of what had just happened to me were the person waiting at the red light opposite me and God.

Later, I heard on TV and read in a few different magazines that the CJ-5 Jeeps were the most dangerous vehicles on the road at that time. Their short wheelbase and the distance between the ground and the frame made them very easy to roll over.

At the time, I thought, *Man, that was cool*, as the Jeep and I hadn't rolled. Not one thing negative had ever happened to me. But truth be known, that had to be the hand of God, and that wasn't the last time God's hand of protection would be on me like that.

A few weeks later, I went over to the house where we usually had parties and where a group of my friends would hang out at. We just called it Jan and Danny's. Danny was a good friend, even if he didn't like to smoke the left-handed cigarettes like just about everybody else who came over to his house. He did like drinking his beers though, and that was cool with me because I had not ever seen him get all ignorant like I had seen a number of other people do before.

On that day, it was a sloppy Friday morning; quite a bit of rain had fallen during the night. So, the supervisors sent us home from the nursery. That was cool with me. An early Friday just meant a longer weekend and that I could spend more time over at Jan and Danny's house, so I did. When I got there, I asked, "Hey, Danny and Robbie"—Robbie was another regular there—"do you guys want to go out east to Wawpecong and do some four wheeling."

They both said, "Sure."

We all got in the Jeep, and I took out a left-handed cigarette to share with Robbie as we headed south. Then we turned on Shannon Road. We drove all the way down until we got to a stop sign. Right in front of us was Route 10. I turned slightly to the right and kept on going straight. I was in first gear and shifted into second and then slowly into third. We were on a dirt road, and the rain had made it sloppy and muddy. On the left-hand side was a small, three-foot high, sloped hill made of all dirt. To me, it looked like a homemade road that some farmer had made as a property divider with a road grader. But the dirt hadn't slid down because it was pretty hard and compacted. The Jeep was moving at a nice, decent speed without any problems. *It's a Jeep, and it has a lift kit on it, along with some nice, fat knobby tires,* I thought. Putting it in four-wheel drive never even crossed my mind. I found out shortly, the hard way, that, if you have a four-wheel drive gear and you're on a road like that, you should use it.

We were slowly cruising down this muddy road, all carefree, well at least I thought we were. All of a sudden, *BAM!* My left front tire hit either a hidden rock that was covered in mud or something that was really hard on that high left side. Whatever it was, we suddenly and totally got flipped around. I don't mean that the Jeep rolled over on us. I mean that we had been going east and suddenly we were facing west.

That reminded me of a passage from the Bible that says, "One thing I know: that though I was blind, now I see" (John 9:25 NKJV). Too bad I had two good, working eyes, and I couldn't see the Hand of God protecting me. I just thought, *Man, once again, I was real lucky.*

Get ready to see one more time the Almighty, protecting Hand of God in action. This time, it was a Friday in mid-October. It had rained during the night, and it was still drizzling during the morning. So our supervisors sent us home from work again.

As we were walking through the parking lot, my cousin, Arthur, asked me, "What are you going to do today?"

I answered, "I'm going over to your house."

"I'll be waiting for you."

First I went home and changed my clothes, and then I told my wife, "I'm going to Arthur's house. I'll be back later."

On my way, I took out one of my left-handed cigarettes and smoked half of it. I felt real nice and mellowed out. So I put it out in the ashtray to save the rest for my cousin. When I got to his place, I got out of my Jeep and knocked at his front door.

His wife answered, and I asked, "Is Arthur here?"

"Yeah," she said. "Come on in."

Arthur was in the living room. "Are you ready to go?" I asked him.

"Yeah," he replied. "Hey, Linda," he said, turning to his wife, "I'll be back later."

With her hand on her hip and leaning slightly toward him, she asked, "Where are you going?"

"With Johnny," he said, as he started looking for a shirt to go out in. "We'll be right back."

"Okay," she replied, walking toward the couch to watch TV, "Don't stay out too late."

"No, we won't be long," he said as he was buttoning up his shirt and grabbing his jacket.

I said, "Come on, man. Let's go."

As we were walking slowly toward the Jeep I asked him, "Do you want to go to The Lucky Star?"

"Yeah, let's go check out Lucinda."

As we both got into the Jeep, I told him, "I left you half a joint in the ashtray."

"Let me see what I can find in here." He took it out and fired it up right away.

Since it was a little chilly outside, we had both of the windows zipped up on the Jeep doors. It didn't take him long before he'd finished the half joint. He unzipped his window and got rid of the little roach.

After we got to The Lucky Star parking lot, we went in. The crowd that usually gathered there hadn't gotten there yet. It was still early in the day, so we had a few quick drinks. Then I said, "Come on, cuz. Let's get out of Dodge."

"Okay," he agreed. "Just let me finish this." He had about half of his drink in front of him still. So he guzzled it down, and out the door we went.

As we were walking toward the Jeep he said, "Let me drive."

"No way, man," I said. "You're drunk."

We both walked over to the driver's side. He kept on insisting he wasn't that drunk.

I finally said, "Okay. But have you ever driven a Jeep before?"

"Sure, it's just like any other car."

I handed him the keys and got in on the passenger's side. Arthur started the Jeep and backed out of the parking lot just fine. We headed south, and his driving seemed normal to me. I told him to turn on the first road going right. He did and was still doing okay. He shifted into first, second, and then third gear. I had been down this road before. It was one of many that I liked to take when I felt like going for a nice, mellow cruise. It was only a few miles long, but it was nice. With plenty of road up in front of us, I asked, "Arthur, can you see the stop sign and that big yellow sign with the arrows on it down at the end of this road?"

He said, "Yeah."

"Well, when we get there, you have to turn left."

"Okay, bro."

As we got closer and closer to the end of the road and the sign, I didn't ever hear him begin to slow down. Before I knew it, we were at the end of the road. I just braced myself with my legs and my arms. I grabbed a hold of a bar that was right in front of me with my right hand

and the dashboard with my left. Neither of us had our seat belts on. I shouted, "Look out!"

And all of a sudden, *BAM!* He drove us through the right leg of that big, yellow sign. An empty cornfield on the other side of the sign made for a little drop-off. So when we went through, the Jeep came to a sudden stop and turned off. I asked him, "Are you okay?"

He looked at me and said, "I hit my mouth on the steering wheel," and stuck his tongue out at me through a slice that was underneath his bottom lip.

I said, "That looks pretty bad, man. I think you need some stitches. Do you want me to take you to the hospital?"

"No, I'm okay."

"All right, but remember that I asked you. Now get out of the Jeep. You can't even drive."

We switched sides, and I turned the Jeep back on. Then I shifted into reverse and slowly drove it back out. As I was driving him home I asked him, "Are you sure you're okay?"

"I'm fine," he insisted.

I said, "All right."

After I drove him home, I went home too. I didn't tell anyone what happened. But early in the morning, our phone rang, and my wife answered it. It was one of Arthur's cousins from his Aunt Consuelo's house, where both he and his wife had spent the night. He was telling my wife that they had taken Arthur to the hospital that night and he wanted me to pay for his bill. My wife told me what he'd said.

I said, "What! I asked him last night quite a few times if he wanted me to take him to the hospital, and he said no. So I'm not paying anything. Let me talk to Arthur."

My wife gave me the phone, and I said, "Put Arthur on the phone." I told him, "I asked you last night if you wanted me to take you to the hospital, and you said no, that you were okay. I would have paid then, but not today."

He said, "No, bro. I didn't ever say I wanted you to pay."

"Okay then. I'll see you later. Bye."

I thought, *Man, this Jeep is a lot of fun, but it can also be very dangerous.*

I didn't even have the slightest idea what was about to happen to me in the near future. Those three incidents that had already happened couldn't even compare to what I would experience about seven months later.

Let me be the one to tell you that life in general had been looking pretty normal—until that special Sunday when a couple of my clients, Sammy and Summer, invited my wife and I over to their place. They had a big-boned female Doberman pinscher with a nice, wide chest that just had puppies. They asked me and my wife, "Would you like one of the puppies?"

We took a look at them and picked the biggest male. Summer told us, "It will be a few weeks before they are weaned off their mother and eating puppy food, but as soon as that happens, I will call and let you know."

After a few weeks went by, the puppy was ready, so Summer called our house and told my wife, "You can drop by to get the puppy anytime."

At that time, I was at Jan and Danny's house and about to go home. Jan had a younger brother named Carl. He was also a client of mine and one of the regulars who hung out there. I asked him, "Do you want to hang out, man?"

He said, "Sure."

On our way to the house, Carl asked me, "Will you go through the Wet Whistle's drive-through so I can pick up a six-pack."

I said, "No problem, man."

We picked it up and popped a couple open as we continued home. When we got there, my wife told me, "Summer called and said we could stop by and pick up the puppy anytime."

So I asked Carl, "Do you want to go with me and get the puppy?"

He said, "Yeah, I'll go with you, but first, do you want to do a line of acid? I got some pink microdot."

Acid, or LSD, is a very bad, heavy-duty hallucinogenic drug that kills brain cells.

Now, I had tried pink microdot once before, by just putting it in my mouth, chewing it really well, and then swallowing. I told him, "I haven't ever tried snorting a pink microdot before, but yeah I'll try it."

"This way it will get to your brain a lot faster and you can feel the effects better," he said, smiling and digging into the front pocket of his shirt. "Do you have anything hard to cut these two hits on?" he asked.

"Yeah, here's a little glass box. You can use the cover."

"Okay, that will work."

After a few minutes, he cut them up and made two lines. He rolled up a dollar bill, snorted one of the lines up, and left me the other one.

I said, "Thanks, man." As he handed me my line, after snorting it up. I told my wife, "I'll be back later. I got to see a man about a dog, literally."

We went downstairs and got into the Jeep. I turned the Jeep and the radio on; what was playing was Bad Company, and we were on our way to Sammy and Summer's house. I turned right coming out of our driveway and then left about a mile and a half down the road. I stayed on that road for a couple of miles, and instead of turning with the road, we had to keep going straight for a little distance because there was a short lane before getting to their house.

On the way over there, I had taken and finished a beer nice and quick. So I laid down the empty bottle right next to my seat, skinny end pointing forward. After being on the road for about fifteen minutes, I could see Sammy and Summer's house in the distance. That particular day, they had company over. So two cars were parked in the driveway, straight in our path. As we were getting to the beginning of their gravel lane and the end of the paved road, I stepped on the clutch and started applying the brakes. My foot sank all the way down to the floorboard. That's when I remembered that my brakes were going bad and I needed to pump on the brake pedal. So I did, but that didn't work. I felt absolutely no resistance on the brake pedal. We flew over a small ditch, and we didn't slow down, not even a little. The driveway was starting to look shorter, and the cars were starting to look closer. So out of instinct alone, I turned the steering wheel toward the right. My right front tire went down a small ditch and flew up. The whole Jeep followed that motion as we went up in the air. All I saw out of the front windshield was blue sky. You know what they say; "What goes up must come down."

And, yes, *BAM!* The Jeep came down and landed on its two left side tires. I turned my head toward the left and looked out my window. All I saw was green grass super close to my face. There was a telephone pole somewhere in front of us, with a wire coming down at an angle from its top, because it was the end pole. The Jeep barely fit sideways between the telephone poll and the wire that was holding it up. Right after we passed through it, the two right side tires came down. In front of us was a barbed wire fence, and the Jeep was still moving toward it at a very slow speed. That's when both Carl and I opened our doors and jumped out.

At the same time, the Jeep ended up stopping, about two feet from the barbed wire fence.

The people inside the house had been looking out the windows while all of this was happening. So they came running out and asked us, "Are you guys okay?"

We said, "Yeah, we always like making an entrance like that."

Okay now, let me try my best to explain what a number of people might consider perfect timing, but still label it as big-time luck. First of all, I thought it was my instincts telling me to turn the steering wheel at that exact time. The empty beer bottle I had put skinny end forward next to my seat, when I hit the ditch was the one that flew under my gas pedal, so it couldn't be pushed down for any reason and make the situation bad. When I hit the ditch with my right front tire, the stick shift flew into neutral. The depth and angle of the ditch was perfect for me to drive the Jeep down into and it to fly up and land on its two left side tires. I held the steering wheel perfectly straight in order to drive the Jeep between the telephone pole and the wire that was holding it on the end. I thank God, from start to finish not one thing went wrong. Everything was perfect. In conclusion, there was no other explanation other than the mighty hand of God was at work once again.

I don't know exactly what chemicals were released in our brains, but after that happened, we were both completely sober. All of that for a puppy, but at least it was free, and we got a chance to talk with some good friends. We ended up safely taking the puppy home, and I eventually fixed the brakes.

CHAPTER 7

THE BEST WAS STILL TO COME

I have always thought that God has shown me special things, big things, and one of those things in particular that will always standout in my mind came on a day that started out looking like any other normal, Summer Friday morning in 1980. I woke up and went to work all day like I usually did, but I didn't do what was normal for me, which was to smoke at least a few joints during the time I was at work. I found it strange that, all day, I never had any desire to light one up. Hando had not found anything worth bringing me; he would only bring me quality merchandise. To me, that meant Mexican red hair sinsemilla.

I always had God on my mind, even if on the back burner. Because I didn't have any marijuana in my possession to sell and because I had never before experienced what in the drug scene is known as a dry spell, I instantly thought that God was trying to tell me something—to get straight with Him, or as I like to put it, stop messing around with the underground.

At the end of the workday, I got my paycheck and went home. After eating supper and taking a nice, cool bath, my wife and I drove to our local Kmart, which was about seven miles away from my parents' house where we were living at that time, and cashed my paycheck. After shopping around for a good two hours, we went home and, to the pleasant surprise of my wife, I had no desire to go out partying like

I had been doing for the first three years of our marriage. I thought, *That has to be God's doing.* After watching a little TV for a few hours, we went to sleep.

At about midnight, the phone woke me up. A good, old friend of mine by the name of Ray was calling. We had known each other since grade school. He explained to me that he had gone out four wheeling at a place we called The Old Indian Burial Grounds in Wilsonville and he had gotten his truck stuck on top of a hill. Now I myself have been out four wheeling plenty of times and wound up on top of a hill. So I couldn't even imagine how he'd gotten his giant, four-wheel drive truck stuck. I thought, *For sure he's been drinking or he's stoned.* But he kept on talking. He wanted to know, "Do you have a chain or a heavy-duty rope to pull me out with?"

I said, "No, but I'll see if my dad has anything around the house."

He said, "I'm at a phone booth outside of a convenience store on Route 30."

"I know the place you're talking about," I said. Turning to look at my wife, I stepped into my pants. "I'll be there in a few minutes," I told him.

I went outside and looked around for something to pull him out with, but after a few minutes of looking, I got a feeling. I couldn't explain it, but I felt God had told me I wasn't going to need a chain or anything.

So I took off in my Jeep and found him exactly where he told me he was going to be. I thought, *Thank God I didn't have a hard time finding him.* After I drove to where he was waiting for me, and he quickly got in.

He asked, "Did you find something to pull me out with?"

I explained how I felt that God had told me I wasn't going to need a chain or anything. I didn't know exactly how we were going to get his giant truck unstuck, but I did know that everything was going to be all right. I asked him, "Why don't you just show me where your truck is?"

As we were driving he asked me, "Do you have anything to smoke?"

I knew he meant marijuana. That's when I told him, "I decided to quit the drugs and drinking altogether—change the channel, in a manner of speaking."

As far as marijuana was concerned, I had my own stash. Every time I got a new load in, I would choose the best of the best and keep it for myself. At the time, I had about a quarter of a pound in a gallon freezer baggie. My intentions were to get rid of it at some time when I was with Ray. When I showed it to him, Ray looked at it with his eyes wide open and asked me, "What are you going to do with this?"

"I'm going to throw it away," I told him.

Now, Ray's eyes opened even wider. "What?" he said. "Don't do that. Let me have it; that's just what the doctor ordered!"

"That sounds like a pretty whacked-out doctor to me. And if I did that," I added, "it would be as if I was poisoning you myself."

He said, "That's all right, man. It won't hurt me; that's just what I need!"

I explained how my giving him the weed I was going to throw away wouldn't be good for him, but he kept on saying, "Come on, man!"

Finally I gave in and said, "Okay. I tried telling you. It's yours."

"All right," he said. "Thanks, man!" He rolled it up and put it inside his jacket.

When we got close to the place where his truck was, we both got out of the Jeep. That's when he took the rolled-up weed from the inside of his jacket and put it down the front of his pants. I could see that he wasn't kidding when he'd said his truck was stuck on top of a hill. We had to park a little distance away from his truck because there was about ten yards of water between us. I could see his big truck stuck on top of a thin hill. To the normal person, this would have looked like an impossible situation. His truck was so long that the giant back tires were not even touching the hill and the two front tires were barely touching the hill. So in a manner of speaking, it was teeter-tottering.

I just looked in disbelief and asked, "How in the world did you do that?"

Ray said, "It wasn't hard man."

"Can the truck move at all?" I asked.

"No," he replied, and started walking over toward his truck. When he got there he showed me how it would just spin its tires. He got out and came back toward me, where I was standing next to my Jeep. Just then, another Jeep pulled up, with two guys who we both knew inside. Ray explained that he had called Jon, who was driving the Jeep. The other guy was named Jerry, and the two hung out together most of the time. My Jeep was a V-6, while Jon's Jeep was a V-8 and a lot stronger; he had also brought a forty-foot, yellow, nylon come-along rope with hooks on both ends—the perfect tools for the job. This showed me that what I had heard from God, about not needing a chain or anything, was true.

Jon gave Ray one end of the come-along rope. Ray hooked it up to the front of his truck, while Jon hooked the other end to the back of his Jeep. I just drove my Jeep out of the way and watched as Jon locked up his two front tires. Ray got in his truck and put it in neutral, as Jon and Jerry got in the Jeep. Jon put it in four high then in drive and floored it. His Jeep was fishtailing about three feet to the left and right. The nylon rope began to stretch. I thought, *For sure it's going to break.* But to my surprise, Ray's truck shot out as if it were in a slingshot. The rope didn't break, and everybody was happy. We all agreed to go home and call it a good night.

On my way home, I was feeling good because everything had turned out better than if I had planned it myself. But the best was still yet to come for me; and even better, the white-cloud adventure had already started. There was a beautiful full moon, with plenty of stars visible in the night sky. I was still about a mile and a half away from my dad's house when something (or maybe I should say Someone) got my attention. I looked up into the night sky over to my right, and I saw something that looked like a white cloud, kind of a light forming in the sky. As I got closer to the house, it got longer and seemed to be following me. I didn't know exactly what it was, but I hadn't ever seen anything like it before. I was both surprised and anxious to know more about that mysterious light.

When I pulled into our driveway, I looked to the right, where we had a large, old, red two-story barn, and the light seemed to stop right over it. A thinner light went straight down on the other side of the barn. Thin lines of light protruded from the large light over the barn and stretched toward the east. I estimated anywhere between seven and eleven of these beams, and they seemed to stretch toward an area nearby us, where two other small towns were located.

I hurried up and got out of my Jeep, and then I walked very quickly into the house. I locked the door behind me and kept on going up the stairs. I took seven long strides that covered three stairs each and made it all the way to the top. I turned sharply to the left and quickly went in our bedroom door. Peering out of our window, which faced the barn toward the east, I told my wife what had just happened. Nothing was there. All of the lights were gone. I wanted to go take a look behind the barn, but it was too late.

I learned an important word that night, and that was *procrastination.* Putting things off for a later time is never the right thing to do. I had never and have never seen anything like that before or after that night, and I wondered what I would have seen, if I would have driven my Jeep toward the back of that barn. I have prayed to God and asked Him to forgive me for my procrastination and to give me another chance—to show me another light like that. But so far, I haven't seen anything even close to what I saw that night, and that's been since 1980.

The incident reminded me of a saying: "Don't put things off for tomorrow that you can do today." Some things in life we only get one chance at, so I believe we should always be ready to just go for it, with precaution of course. Hope, pray, and believe that whatever situation presents itself to you is from God. It may be something out of the ordinary, and it may even give you the heebie-jeebies. The way I once heard it put was, "If fear comes a knocking, send faith to answer, and no one will be there."

Now I have to admit, that was something surprising and big, really big— something you don't see every night. That straightened me out for a good three weeks. I started getting into the Bible. I read the Psalms, and I liked the feeling I got. I started getting rid of some of the things I thought were not pleasing to the Lord. I wanted God to be happy with me. I thought, *For sure, I have to get rid of these books on the occult and anything else dealing with the occult.* So I gathered up my small collection of books and took them outside to the burning barrel and started a fire with them. I also had a large picture of a woman barely clothed from around the knights and wizards era. A very small part of her breasts and between her legs was covered in some kind of ancient armor, and she had long, flowing, blond hair. She was between two large komodo dragons on a felt canvas that was about three and a half feet long by two and a half feet wide. The fire was going pretty good, so I threw the felt canvas in. That's when I remembered I had a Ouija board put away that we hadn't used for a while. So I ran upstairs and got it.

When I brought it down and threw it in, out of nowhere, a big ball of fire flew up. And I kid you not, it was there only for an instant, but it was in the shape of a face with horns and a pointy beard, with eyes and everything else. I thought, *Wow, man, and I had that in the house in our room.* But it was daylight, so I didn't even give it a second thought.

One Saturday after work, after I'd been clean from all the negative stuff for three weeks, I was reading my Bible. I got this idea that I should start reading from the very beginning, where God talks about creation; at least I thought it was my idea. When I read, "And God said, Behold, I have given you every herb bearing seed, which is upon the face of all the earth" (Genesis 1:29 KJV), my thinking started to change. I kept reading. In verse 30, "And to everything that creepeth upon the earth, wherein there is life, I have given every green herb for meat: and it was so." I checked those words out, and without even asking anybody what the passages might mean. I concluded that, according to verse 29, God had made herb for man, so it was okay for me to have herb and to sell it. From what I understood in verse 30, He made herb for everything that had life, and I was alive, and so were all my clients. The clincher for me was verse 31—"And God saw everything that He had made, and, behold, it was very good." My thinking was, *If God says it's very good, then that means it's very good.* So the guilt was gone for me.

I see now how the devil works. He's sly. I believe he's the one who put the idea in my head about starting from the very beginning of the Bible. I surely did not pass that test.

At about that same time, Hando called and told me he was over at Lucinda's. I told him, "I'll be over there in a little bit."

When I got to Lucinda's, I parked right next to his truck, walked in, and sat across from him at the table he was at.

He said, "I have something with me." I knew what he was talking about. Then he asked me, "Where did you park?"

I told him, "I parked right next to your truck."

Lucinda came over to our table and asked me, "What do you want to drink?"

"I'll have a Jack and Coke," I told her.

Hando still had half of his beer left. After we finished our drinks, Hando said, "Let's go outside."

When we got out there, he said, "Open your Jeep door." I had parked my Jeep backward, so my driver's side door was right next to his. I'd thought when he called me, *It's about time for Hando to come up with a load*, and, bingo, my guesstimation was right. He opened up his truck door, leaned the back of his seat forward, and grabbed a black plastic garbage bag that had some bundles of mota in it and passed it over to me.

I put it behind my seat. "Okay," I told him. "We'll talk later on." We both fixed our seats and drove away.

When I got home, I got out of the jeep and took the bag from behind my seat. After closing it up really well, I ran upstairs into our bedroom. I had a nice-sized plastic tablecloth that I would unfold on our floor; I'd put all the bundles of mota on it, just in case someone knocked on our door and I had to put it away real quick. The setup also allowed me to gently and carefully pull the bundles apart without making a mess all over the place. After I pulled a few of the bundles apart, I could see and smell that it was the same Mexican red hair sinsemilla. But I could still see quite a few seeds in the shake. I saw the red hairs in the mota, along with a few other nice-looking colors.

I tried it, and it did have the same Missouri mule kick. But the word *sinsemilla* means "without seed in Spanish" I felt obligated to ensure that the mota lived up to its name. After separating the shake from the buds, I would take a pack of my rolling papers and use the thin part to clean the seeds from the shake, so the shake would be seedless. That way, the only seeds would be in the buds. The way I thought was, *If I'm getting nine hundred dollars a pound, five hundred for half, and two hundred fifty for a quarter, then I need to do a little extra.* That's why all of my clients were always satisfied.

It didn't take long before I was all sold out.

There were a couple of times when I got some new stuff in and it seemed a little dry, but Hando always told me before I even saw it, "Make sure to mix in some cabbage leaves or orange peels with the mota in order to bring it back to life because these loads are a little dry." With a little trial and error, I found out that orange peels worked the best. After I had carefully separated apart the bundles and taken peels off five large oranges, I'd get a large plastic garbage bag and put some orange peels on the bottom. Then I'd add about a foot of mota, followed by some more orange peels in the middle. I'd put more mota on top of that, and finally, I'd add the last layer of orange peels on top and tie the bag up. I'd make sure to check it every day to see if the mota had been rejuvenated. Once the orange peels had done their job and given CPR to the mota, in a manner of speaking, I would carefully go through the bag and take out the orange peels to prevent mold from starting to grow. I didn't ever once get any complaint about anything anyone got from me.

One normal-looking Saturday in late spring, a client of mine, who had his own construction company, called and asked, "Half you ever tried an apple pie from McDonald's?"

Just in case someone may have been listening over the telephone, he made it sound like he was asking a normal every day question.

I knew what he meant when he asked that; it was his way of letting me know he wanted a half pound.

As per our code, I responded simply, "Yes."

"I like the size, taste, and flakiness, and I'm going to be stopping by the McDonald's on Maple Street in Kewanee for lunch," he replied.

"What time are you going to take your lunch break?" I asked.

"At eleven thirty."

"Okay, I'll see you there."

At eleven thirty, I drove to McDonald's and saw Jeffrey's car parked in the parking lot, so I parked right next to it. I left the large, brown paper bag with the half pound of mota there in the Jeep and walked in. As I looked over toward the left and saw Jeff sitting alone at a booth eating a hamburger, I walked over there and sat with him. "Hey, Jeff," I said.

He said, "Hey, Johnny. I bought an apple pie to go with my lunch."

"That sounds like a good deal to me."

"Do you want anything to eat or drink?" he asked.

"I said, "No, thanks."

He reached in the right back pocket of his blue jeans and handed me a McDonald's fry bag. I took it and looked inside. When I saw some money in it, I put the fry bag in the inside pocket of my black leather jacket.

"It's all there," he said.

After he finished his lunch, he asked, "So do you have the stuff in your Jeep?"

"Yes, in a brown paper bag."

"Let's get out of here. I'll get in my car and pop the trunk open; you get in your Jeep and toss the bag in my trunk."

"That'll work for me."

Jeff had a fancy-looking car. Once he got in the driver seat, he did something, and the trunk slowly started opening. I unzipped my window, turned the Jeep on, shifted it into reverse, and backed up until I was about even with his trunk. I grabbed the bag and tossed it in his trunk. He did something else, and the trunk started to slowly close by itself. Once I saw that happening, I pulled out of the parking lot, turned the radio on, and headed home. Playing on the radio was, "Another One Bites the Dust."

The next day around noon, I got a phone call. It was another client of mine named Michael. He asked, "Hey, Johnny, are you busy, or do you have time to come over so we can talk?"

"No, I'm not busy," I told him. "I'll be over in a few minutes."

After we hung up, I told my wife, "I have to go see a man about a dog real quick. I'll be back after a little while."

Michael was renting a farmhouse out in the country. It was a nice little ride for me. I liked the scenery. When I arrived, I got out of my Jeep and knocked on his front door.

"Come in, Johnny," he said.

"Hey, Michael, what's happening, man?"

"Not too much," he replied. "What I wanted to talk to you about is I know I owe you some money. I don't have the money to pay you right now. So I wanted to know if you would take some of these things I have here for the money I owe you."

"Well, let's see what you've got."

"I have this nice .45-caliber Smith & Wesson. It comes with this shoulder holster that has two extra clip holders. I'll throw in the two extra clips. I also have this comfortable, white swivel chair. You can use it to watch TV or whatever you want. Maybe just sit in it and listen to this stereo I have right here. It's a Kenwood. It has these two big speakers, a record player, a cassette player, a radio, and an equalizer. It all sits in this glass case that has all this extra room down here. Oh and I also have this M1 rifle. I have a few extra rounds for the both of them. We can go behind the barn, and you can try them out if you want."

I told him, "I haven't ever seen an M1 rifle before; let's go check them out."

We took the guns and a couple of tin cans out to the barn with us. After I tried the guns out, I asked him, "Are the guns or any of this stuff hot?"

"No," he assured me. "These are all my things. I just want to get you squared away."

"Okay, I'll take all these things for what you owe me," I said. "I'll have to come back with a truck and a couple of guys to help me load this stuff up."

I drove over to Vinnie's house and walked up to his front door and knocked His wife, Susie, answered.

I said, "Hi, Susie, is Vinnie here?"

"Yeah, come on in," she said. Susie yelled down into the basement, "Hey, Vinnie, Johnny is here to see you!"

Vinnie came up the stairs and said, "Hey, Johnny. What's up, man?"

"I need you and Freddie's help to go get some things from Michael's house."

"Let's go take care of that."

I asked, "Do you know if Freddie's home?"

"I just saw him over at his house a little while ago. I'm pretty sure he's still there."

"Well, let's go check him out."

Vinnie got in the Jeep with me, and we drove to Freddie's house. When we got there, we both got out of the Jeep. I knocked on his front door.

Freddie said, "Come in."

Vinnie and I walked in, and Freddie was at his kitchen table rolling a joint. I said, "Hey, Freddie, I need you to come with us over to Michael's and help me load some of his stuff up. He owes me some money. He doesn't have it, and it's time to pay the fiddler. Before we go over there, I need to stop at my dad's house."

Freddie said, "Let's fire this up first."

Vinnie said, "Now that sounds like a good idea to me. Pass it over, man."

After we finished the joint and threw the little roach away, I drove us over to my dad's house. I asked him, "Can I borrow your truck for a few hours? This guy I know is going to give me a few things, and I'll bring it back as soon as I'm done with it."

He said, "Sure."

Vinnie, Freddie, and I drove to Michael's house and loaded up everything Michael and I had agreed on.

Vinnie said, "If you don't want this stereo, we can drop it off at my house; this looks nice, man."

I said, "Be patient, and you'll be able to get one of these for yourself."

As soon as we were done loading everything, I took out one of my left- handed cigarettes. I said, "Now we can fire this bad boy up."

A few months later, things in terms of finances started going a lot better for both Michael and Jeff. They knew each other, and they both knew me. So they decided to combine minds and resources. After I got off work one Thursday, Michael called me and said, "Jeff and I need to talk with you about something."

"Okay. I'll be over at your place at seven thirty," I told him.

When I got to Michael's house, I saw Jeff's car was already there. I got out of my Jeep and knocked on his door. Michael said, "Come in, Johnny."

"Hey, Jeff, you beat me here, man. How have you guys been doing?" I asked.

Jeff said, "Great! That's why I wanted to get together and ask you if you know of someone down in Texas who you can buy some stuff from and how much money you would need."

"Yes, I do," I told him. "Do you have at least ten grand together, or can you get it?"

"Yes, I can get it together," Jeff said. "As much stuff as you can get down there with the ten grand I will pay for."

Michael added, "We can drive my car down there. I will pay for the gas and whatever food we eat. We can take Vinnie with us, and he can help us drive. That way, we can drive straight down and back without stopping, and you can be back to work on Monday."

"Okay," I agreed. "That sounds like a plan, man." I was relying on my knowledge of both people down in South Texas and people up in Illinois who had money instead of God Almighty. Slowly but surely, I started to pray less and less to God, believing I didn't really need His help as much, (big mistake).

I made a phone call to a man I knew who sold mota. I asked him, "Have you been eating any fresh fruit from around there, or is it even the season for fresh fruit?"

"Yeah, I have an orange tree in my front yard and two valley lemon trees that are both full of fruit," he told me.

"That's great; I'll talk to you on Saturday."

I called Jeff and told him, "Everything is all set up for Saturday. So Friday after I get off work, we take off. You talk to Michael, and I'll talk to Vinnie."

When I spoke with Vinnie, I said, "Are you ready to roll tomorrow. After I get off work, we're going to ride with Michael down to Texas and pick up some mota. Just think of it as a paid vacation, and you can help us drive, man. We can just have Freddie drop us off at Michael's tomorrow."

Vinnie said, "Cool, you just give me a call, and I'll get a hold of Freddie. I'll tell him tonight, so he'll be ready tomorrow."

"Sounds cool, man. I'll talk to you tomorrow."

Everything went according to plan, smooth as silk. We took off from Illinois on Friday evening, and Saturday we were in Texas. Because of what I had seen, like where the stuff could safely be placed for the long haul, I was able to comment and show them some good places to put it. Monday morning before it was time to punch my time card, I was there ready for work.

After a couple of months went by, I could see that money didn't have any real value for Michael and me. It seemed too easy to go down and come back up. Or if someone brought me some stuff to sell, it felt like the thrill was gone. It seemed as common as putting my pants on in the morning. I usually didn't go to any of the bars in Kewanee or in Williamsville. I would usually just go to The Lucky Star, because it was close by on the outskirts of Pleasant Park. I have no idea why, on this special Saturday night, the place that came to mind was a bar in Williamsville by the name of The Last Call. I had only been there once before with some friends. This time, I was by myself.

When I walked in, I saw Michael playing pool, and it was real close to closing time. When he saw me, he said, "Hey, Johnny, come over here. We have time for just one game of pool. You rack them up, and I'll play you for a grand or a pound of the stuff we deal with."

I'm no Minnesota Fats by any means, but I've never been one to back down from a friendly pool game. When it came to witnesses around the table, there were none. So I said okay. I won that game.

Later on, I found out that my friend, Ray, along with two other guys who he knew, had rented a nice, two-story house with a furnished basement that had a real nice pool table. It was in Williamsville. I went over there a few times, and we had some very interesting pool games. Some I won, and some I lost. What I noticed is, because of the quality of the mota and its value, handling it became an everyday, normal thing for me.

After a while, I began to think to myself, *I haven't ever seen quantity, but since the very beginning I have always seen quality. I thank God I didn't ever become addicted to the stuff.* I will have to admit, if I ever ran into a dry spell (which wasn't very often), I couldn't really explain it, but I just didn't feel normal. I felt edgy and irritated, and my patience was even less than usual. It wasn't because I was hooked on the stuff and I didn't have any, as I usually had my own personal stash and didn't mind sharing. But I still had that empty feeling inside that I just didn't like.

I remember one specific time when a dry spell I hadn't anticipated came. It didn't last very long, thank God. I was all out of my personal stash, and it was a Friday night. After I took care of some things at home, I went over to Jan and Danny's house. When I got there, I saw the usual handful of people who gathered there. I asked, "Does anybody know where I can get some good weed?"

Carl quickly answered, "Yeah, Sammy and Summer have some Colombian Gold for sale, but it's real expensive. I think they're the only ones that have anything in town right now."

"Cool. Let's go get us a quarter pound."

After we got it, I cleaned it up really well. I said to myself, *It's been a while since I've had anything besides Mexican sinsemilla, so I better roll a decent-sized joint.* I put about six rolling papers together, and I rolled up the whole quarter pound, in one giant joint. It looked like something out of a Cheech & Chong movie. At the end, everybody was super buzzed—not that I remember. But I was told by Danny the next day, because he kept an eye on us. When we were all sitting around at his big dinner table, some people just started getting up and walked out without even saying anything to anybody. Others just slouched down in the chair they were sitting in and fell asleep with their mouths open. I don't even remember getting up and driving home that night. But Danny said, "You told everybody you were leaving and you would see them tomorrow." I really don't believe I even prayed that night.

The next day was Saturday, and around ten thirty in the morning, I told my wife, "I'm going over to Jan and Danny's house. I'll be back later."

When I got there, I asked Jan, "Where is Danny?"

"He went to get something in Kewanee, but he should be right back," she answered, wiping her glasses with her shirt. She turned around and headed back to the kitchen.

Then one of the regulars who hung around there, Lana, said, "I just got some acid in a blotter form."

I later found out that ACID/LSD can come in both a blotter or a microdot form and that it can be a heavy-duty hallucinogenic drug. It all depends on the amount of drops of LSD put on each square or microdot.

Lana asked, "Does anybody want to check out some acid?"

I had no idea what I was about to get myself into. I had tried this in a microdot form, which was not very potent. I would soon find out that this stuff was very fresh. I said, "Let me see what you got there." She took out a small sheet of paper from inside of a baggie with a bunch of little precut squares on it, and each square had a picture of Mickey Mouse in a wizard costume. He was waving a magic wand that had stars coming out of the tip. I thought, *That looks like a nice, little picture.*

I asked, "Is this supposed to cop me a buzz?"

"This will keep you going for about eleven hours," she told me.

With a little doubt in my mind, I asked, "For how long? Let me try one of those. So what do I do first?"

"Put it in your mouth and chew it up really good." I said, "Okay." It had no taste.

She asked everybody there, "Does anybody else want to trip?" About five other people also said they wanted to trip.

I looked at her and said, "I don't feel anything. Now what?" Giggling, she said, "Swallow it and wait about twenty minutes."

After the twenty minutes went by, we were all sitting in the living room just talking normal. All of a sudden, *BAM!* Once again it felt like a Missouri Mule had just kicked me on the back of my head. But at least this time I had a little bit of a warning. What I remember about that night is the room was real dark. I was talking with someone who was sitting on the couch with me. All night, they kept asking me if I wanted to sell my soul to the devil, and then that same person would laugh. I would answer, "No," and clap my hands, and she would stop laughing. I could feel a heavy, thick, evil presence there but no fear. I turned it into a game where I'd clap and make my tripping buddy laugh and then clap to make her stop again. That kept going on for quite a while that night.

Finally, the sun came up, and all during the night and part of the morning nobody had eaten or drank hardly anything. The couple of times that I had tried to drink something, it hadn't tasted good at all.

After the sun came up, my mouth felt like it was full of cotton, and I had a taste of spoiled milk in my mouth; it was nasty. In the morning, I spoke with Lana.

She said, "When we were sitting on the couch talking and laughing last night, all of a sudden, you started speaking in an unknown language that was not Spanish or English."

To me, it felt like an intense adventure, even after going through all those things and eventually finding out that LSD could stay in your system for up to a year or more and that you could have a flashback from one of the times you had done acid. I later found out that acid is one of the worst drugs out there and it can kill brain cells. I need to keep as many of those as possible. But not even that stopped or discouraged me from looking for the next trip. I remember pulling a few all-nighters.

Most of my LSD trips were good. I did have a few that were pretty hairy, and most of those times, I didn't make time to pray. Slowly but surely, I was straying further away from God.

CHAPTER 8

MAGIC OR ALMIGHTY GOD?

Once Mary and I moved out on our own, I started seeing a number of the things I had asked for when I was dabbling with witchcraft come to fruition for me, even after I'd burned all the books.

First, when I initially got hired on at the nursery, I didn't want to get laid off for the wintertime, like most people usually did. And my supervisors didn't lay me off.

Second, I didn't want to do the regular nursery stuff that gets done during the wintertime, like preparing the plants for planting during the upcoming springtime. I thought that was boring and somewhat of a dirty job, and I didn't have to do that either. Instead, I was instructed to help some carpenters who the nursery had hired; that work lasted for a few months. I really liked helping the carpenters out, I learned a lot, and I didn't even get half as dirty.

Third, one of the things I had specifically asked for was to have special privileges. Since the carpenters only took a half-hour break for lunch and didn't take the two extra fifteen-minute breaks I was used to, I would get off half an hour earlier than the rest of the people at the nursery. Being able to punch my time card half an hour earlier and still have all my time in for the day like everybody else—now that made me feel special.

Fourth, I had asked for love. I had just gotten married to a beautiful, young Latin lady. But I still wanted more. It seemed like, when it came to sex, I just couldn't get enough. In the Bible it's called lasciviousness. What I had specifically asked for was for young females to desire me and want to be with me. I wasn't talking about them standing up close to me either. Shortly after I asked for that, I started to notice that just about everybody wanted to hang around me, especially young females who were in the circle I was a part of.

Initially, I didn't think anything of it because I still had my doubts about magic really working. Eventually, I noticed and thought it was awkward that the young females wanted to get really close when they were talking to me and kept staring at me. At first, I thought they were just interested in what I had to say. But then I kept on getting bumped into, and afterward the girls would smile and giggle at me. I later found out that it was all part of the flirting. Once I discovered the girls were interested in me and not just my conversation, I took it to the next level, and for me that meant sex. Initially I thought, *Man, I just got married*, so I felt a little guilty.

After a while, I noticed other females who weren't a part of my immediate circle act the same way, so I thought, *It's on.* Slowly but surely, my blister became a callous. It didn't bother me anymore. My morality and ethics became a thing of the past.

Fifth, I had asked for money, and that's when I met my cousin Arthur and company, in a manner of speaking. The merchandise that was usually available to me 24-7 was fresh and potent and had a kick like a Missouri mule. That made it easier to not feel bad about what I was doing. And to top it off, I didn't mind trying many different kinds of alcoholic beverages. Being under the influence of some sort of high-quality drug or a little alcohol at times was like the cherry on top of the cake for me. I was usually firing one up, and if I knew you, I didn't mind sharing.

My mind had gotten perverted and was becoming more and more wicked as the days went by. That word *wicked* comes from the word *wicker*, which means "twisted," like wicker furniture. Wicker is furniture made from bent and twisted branches. Originally, a branch may be fairly straight, but with manipulation (bending and twisting), you can change the shape of the branch in a way it wasn't originally. In my case, my manipulation was the people I decided to associate with and then the things I started doing. Even the way I spoke changed big-time. I really, honestly thought that I wasn't doing anything wrong. One passage in the Bible, in the book of Hosea, says, "My people are destroyed for lack of knowledge" (Hosea 4:6 KJV).

I was making available the best marijuana around for a below-average price. In my ignorance, I believed I was helping people out so they could have a chance to try some really good quality merchandise they might not ever get a chance to see outside of a magazine. Initially, I was willing to take a chance on even people I didn't know all that well. I would let them take it without paying me until after they had sold the merchandise. That most definitely was one of the things I changed after becoming an old dog in this business, in a manner of speaking. My intentions were never to hurt anyone. I was just having the time of my life, (at least that's what I thought). I wanted everybody else to have the same opportunity to try some super great-quality merchandise.

Most of the time it was sinsemilla that I had for sale. Only a couple of times, when I ran into a dry spell with marijuana, did I ever dabble with cocaine. When it came to marijuana, each new batch I got in would be a little different-looking. The color might be a little darker or sometimes lighter, but it always had plenty of red hair.

One day after I got off work, it was summertime in the middle of the month of June, our phone rang. The voice on the other end of the line asked, "Is this Johnny?"

I said, "Yes."

"My name is Emilio," the caller said. "I'm a friend of Hando's. Do you remember me?"

"Yes, I do."

"Hando told me you worked with him before. I have something to show you. It's not what you're used to seeing. Have you ever had dandruff before?"

"Yes."

"You know what I'm talking about right."

"Yes, that white stuff that comes out of your hair from your head."

"Yeah. Why don't you come to my motel room so we can talk? I'm staying at the Plaza Inn on Main Street in room number eleven."

I said, "I'll see you in a few minutes."

Before I drove to where Emilio was staying, I made a quick phone call to my friend, Eric. We just called him the Professor because of the glasses he wore. I asked him, "Can you go for a ride with me?"

He said, "Yeah. Where we going?"

"I'll tell you when I get there," I told him.

I pulled into his driveway and honked the horn. He walked out of his house and jumped into my Jeep. He said, "Hey, Johnny. What's up?"

"Hey, Eric, I need your expertise, man. You know more about cocaine than I do, and I have to go see a man in Kewanee at the Plaza Inn on Main Street."

I drove into the Plaza Inn parking lot, we got out, and I said, "Number eleven, right here."

I knocked, and Emilio answered the door. He asked, "Who is this?"

"He's a friend of mine. He's cool."

Emilio took a good, hard look into Eric's eyes for a couple of seconds, and then he said, "Okay, come in and sit down."

A small, round table sat in the middle of the room. We grabbed a chair and sat down, while Emilio went over to the closet and came back with a small, brown paper bag. He opened it up and pulled out a small plastic baggie and put it in the middle of the table. He said, "Take a look at this." This was the first time I had ever seen an ounce of cocaine all at the same time. I thought, *Cool. So that is what cocaine is supposed to look like.* It was in the shape of a rock, about the size of a lady's small fist, with a little bit of loose powder at the bottom in a small baggie. He took out a razor blade, opened the baggie, and cut off a piece from the rock. He put it on a small mirror that was on the table, chopped it up finely, and made three lines. He opened his wallet and took out a twenty-dollar bill. He rolled it up and snorted the line that was closest to him. Next, he passed Eric the rolled up bill, scooted the mirror close to him, and said, "Try it." Eric did the same and passed it over to me.

Emilio had some beer in a little cooler with some ice that he offered us. The evening turned to night, and eventually, morning came around. Before we knew it, we had been there for twelve hours, going around and around with that little mirror. I had not ever done so much cocaine at one time in my life.

Emilio said, "If you want, I'll leave this with you. And here is some good cut, so you can put in what is missing." (*Cut* is the word for any substance you mix in with the cocaine to make it weigh more.) I found out after I weighed the remainder of the cocaine at home on my triple beam scale that we had done eight grams of good, high quality coke.

It was not hard to sell. It was some of the best stuff in town. I thank God that, in a matter of no time, it had all been sold. I can see how some people get very easily used to having that kind of stuff around, (or get hooked on it). It could take over your life if you're not careful.

After some time had passed by, I slowly began to meet and talk to new people. Depending on how well I knew the person who had introduced me to the new people and whether I got good vibes from them or if I felt we were in the appropriate place, I would usually fire up one of my left-handed cigarettes.

Sixth, and last but not least, I had asked for protection against the police. I don't know exactly how the local cops had found out I was dealing drugs. But they were constantly watching me and trying to catch me with something incriminating on me so they could arrest me. Out of all the books I had read, one other book that especially caught my eye dealt with mind control. And that was in addition to the things I had already learned from the first book, *The Magic Power in You*. I had already practiced and proven a lot of the things from it.

I remember the first time I really tried what I had read in the book on mind control. It was a chilly Thursday evening after I had just gotten off work. On my way home, I saw Ray driving his truck in our little town of Pleasant Park. So we both stopped in the middle of the road and opened our windows. He asked me, "So did you just get off work?"

I said, "Yeah, where are you headed to?"

"Nowhere really. Do you want to get together?"

"Yeah, I haven't been home yet. But if you want, I'll see you in about an hour. I'll pick you up at your place."

He said, "All right, man. Later."

"Later."

When I went to pick him up, I stopped outside of his place. I parked the Jeep, knocked on his door, and went in. I said, "Hey, Ray, are you ready to go for a cruise?"

He said, "Yeah, man, let's go. Do you have any smoke on you?"

"Yeah, a little bit."

After we both got in my Jeep, I turned both it and the heater on. I reached inside my coat pocket and took out a baggie. But I only had one of my left-handed cigarettes rolled up in it. I started driving toward Red Oaks Park. I handed Ray the baggie and told him to fire it up. He took the joint out of the baggie and did just that. He took a couple of good hard hits off it before he passed it over to me. It didn't take us long before we got to the park. I drove around it one time and then pulled over on the west side of the park. We were still hitting on that left-handed cigarette, passing it back and forth. I took a good, hard hit off it and looked out my window at the same time. To my surprise, there was a police car that had stopped right beside my Jeep on the road. The policeman driving was watching me take a serious hit off the joint.

I inconspicuously handed it over to Ray underhand as I kept looking straightforward. I said, "There's a cop right beside us. Get rid of this."

Ray unzipped his window a little and threw it out, just as the policeman parked his car right behind us. He slowly got out of his car and came to the side by my window. Then he motioned and said, "Unzip the window."

The combination of Ray's window being barely unzipped open and my unzipping my window all the way down suddenly produced a wall of smoke that—*BAM!*—hit the policeman right in the face.

The policeman asked, "Can I see your driver's license?"

So I pulled my license out of my wallet and gave it to him.

While he was looking at it he asked, "What are you two doing here?"

I said, "Nothing. We were just sitting here talking, enjoying the night."

"Have you been smoking any marijuana, because it smells like cannabis?"

"No, sir," I told him.

"Do you mind if I look in the Jeep?"

"No, go ahead."

As I was getting out of the Jeep, he asked, "Can I pat you down?"

I said, "Sure."

After he was done patting me down and looking in the ashtray, he told Ray to step out of the Jeep and walk toward the back. He looked underneath the seat, underneath the floor mat, in the spot where the seat bent forward, and finally, he looked in the area behind the seat. He asked Ray, "Can I pat you down?"

He said, "Sure."

After he got done, he told Ray, "I found this empty baggie on your side, and it smells like cannabis."

"I don't know anything about that; it's not mine."

"Okay, I'm not going to put the cuffs on you two, but you can go get in my car because it's a little chilly out here."

Ray got in the passenger seat, and I got in the backseat.

The policeman went back and looked again on my side. He went over to Ray's side and came back to the car. He started writing on a sheet of paper that was on his clipboard. He said, "I didn't find anything in the Jeep. But on the passenger side right outside the door, on top of the snow, I did find a small piece of unsmoked marijuana cigarette. It looked undisturbed, like it had just gotten placed there."

I said, "We don't know anything about that, and we don't have anything on us. The only thing we were doing here was talking."

He radioed for a backup to come to Red Oaks Park, along with a tow truck. He told me and Ray, "I'll be right back. I have to go get a number off the Jeep."

Ray said, "We are so busted, man!"

I said, "Calm down. Everything is going to be okay."

"Didn't you hear him? He called for another police car and a tow truck to come pick up your Jeep!"

"Everything will be all right; he's going to let us go." Ray said, "But you just heard him on the radio."

The policeman returned with his clipboard in hand and sat down. I concentrated on a certain spot on the back of his head, like I remembered the book said to do. Zeroing in only on that spot, I thought hard, over and over, *You want to let us go. You do not want to take us in.*

Out of the blue, the policeman said, "I'll tell you what; if the two of you can promise me never to come back to this park again and you can get out of here before the other police car and the tow truck get here, you're free to go."

I said, "Okay, we promise."

Ray said, "Yeah, we promise."

He said, "Okay, get out of here."

I told Ray, "Hurry up and open my door."

He scrambled out and opened my door.

I said, "Now hurry up and get in the Jeep."

Ray said, "How did you know he was going to let us go?"

As we were driving away, I told him I had read a book on mind control and I had put an idea in the policeman's mind. I told Ray, "That's pretty cool, man; this stuff really works."

I turned on the radio, and we listened to "Slow Ride" on our way back to his house.

The next day after work, I made a couple quarter-pound sales. I noticed that I had run out of all the merchandise I had for sale, and my stash was pretty low. Hando called me on the telephone and said, "I'm not going to be able to come see you because I'm going to be busy with some things I have to take care of."

I said, "Okay. Have you seen or eaten any lemon limes, I mean valley lemons? We have some lemons around here, but they can't even compare to the valley lemons."

He knew what I meant by that. He said, "You should come down here and get some. You could come on the weekend. I always fly Continental. If you do that, you could get here in a few hours, and then you could drive my truck back."

"Okay, I'll do that."

It was a Thursday. I told my wife, "I'll be back later; I'm going over to Vinnie's." Vinnie was a good, trustworthy friend of mine who'd helped me a number of times in many ways; all I had to do was ask.

He must have heard me pull into his driveway, because he came out right away and got in my Jeep. He said, "Hey, Johnny, what's going down, man?"

"Not too much yet. I just got done talking with Hando, and he said he can't come up because he has to take care of some things but suggested that I fly down this weekend. Do you want to come with me?"

"Yeah," Vinnie said. "I've never flown in an airplane before."

"That's okay. Neither have I."

Freddie was another friend who had my back all the time. If I ever needed him for anything, he was always ready to go. They both lived out in the country, on the outskirts of Pleasant Park. I told Vinnie, "Let's go talk to Freddie." He only lived a few houses away from Vinnie.

We pulled into his driveway and got out of the Jeep. I knocked on his door, and he answered. I said, "Hey, Freddie, what's up, man?"

"Not much. Come on in."

Vinnie asked, "Do you have any smoke?"

He said, "I'm tearing apart my roaches right now." (For those of you not familiar with those words, in the drug lingo, that means to tear apart the small, leftover end pieces of your marijuana cigarettes in order to roll up a new joint with the leftovers). "We'll have us something to smoke in a few minutes."

After he got done with the roaches he had and rolled them up, I told Freddie, "That's okay, keep your stuff. Here, turn this on."

They knew that, whenever I rolled one of my left-handed cigarettes, it was always a nice, little stogie. When it came down to rolling joints, I didn't like messing around. Freddie turned it on, hit it nice and hard, and passed it to me.

I took a couple good, hard hits and passed it over to Vinnie. We kept that going while I told Freddie, "Vinnie and I need you to give us a ride to O'Hare tomorrow. After I get off work, we're going to fly down to the valley and pick up some weed. We'll be back before I have to go in to work on Monday."

Freddie said, "All Right! We need some new stuff because there isn't anything anywhere."

The next day came and went, nice and fast. I took care of everything I needed to take care of before I called Freddie and told him to go pick up Vinnie and then come by the house. I told my wife, "I'm not going to be around for a couple of days because I have to go see a man about a dog. If anybody asks about me, just tell them I'm not home. But let them know that, as soon as you see me, you'll give me the message."

When Freddie and Vinnie got there, I asked them, "Are you guys ready to go?"

They both said, "Yeah."

I already had everything I needed with me, so I said, "Let's hit the road." I turned toward my wife and said, "I'll see you later, babe."

We all got in Freddie's car. Vinnie had a map so we 'wouldn't get lost on the way to the airport. Freddie dropped us off curbside. I hadn't ever been to an airport before, and O'Hare Airport seemed to be very busy. Vinnie and I just looked for the sign that would direct us to the Continental airline. We walked up to the ticket counter, and I asked the lady, "When is the next flight to South Texas scheduled?"

She said, "There's a flight scheduled to MacAllen Texas, and it's going to leave in twenty minutes from gate 112."

"That sounds great. I need two one-way tickets."

I bought two tickets and handed Vinnie his. The ticket lady pointed us toward gate 112.

I told Vinnie, "Come on; let's hurry."

It didn't take us long at all before we found gate 112. The flight wasn't boarding yet, so we had a little extra time. It reminded me of what I had seen on TV when people had to wait before going to board on an airplane. Shortly, we heard a lady announce over the intercom "Flight 107 to MacAllen Texas is boarding at gate 112."

I told Vinnie, "Hey, that's us, man."

We got in line and handed the lady our tickets. We walked onto the airplane and found our seats. I had the window seat, and Vinnie had the aisle seat.

After everyone had boarded the plane, one of the stewardesses came on the intercom and said, "Good evening. Welcome to Continental flight 107 to MacAllen Texas. Glad to have you on board. Everyone, sit back, relax, and buckle your seatbelts because we're about to take off."

At first, it was a little rough going down the runway. But once we got off the ground, the plane felt super smooth. And then, when we touched back down for the landing, it was the opposite. Vinnie and I hadn't ever felt anything like that before, but everything was cool.

When we got off the plane, Hando was waiting for us, as I'd called him when we were waiting to board the plane and told him to pick us up at 11:15. He asked, "So how was your flight?"

As we were walking, I told him, "It was fine, and they gave us a little something to eat plus all the peanuts we wanted." We both laughed. Whenever I spoke with Hando, it was always in Spanish. I'm sure he knew how to speak English a little, but he didn't ever speak it with me.

He said, "I drove this car to the airport to pick you guys up, and I'll take you to where the truck is ready to go." He reminded me of the first time I helped him cut the spare tire open. That's where he was carrying the bundles of mota that time. He said, "This time, I put them in the door panels."

I said, "That's cool."

As we headed to his truck, Hando told us, "There's only one checkpoint, and that's in Hernandez County, about three towns away from where the truck is. As long as they see you act normal, not nervous, there shouldn't be a problem with them letting you drive straight through the checkpoint. Usually, they just wave you straight through, or they might ask you to pull over to the side and question you about being a United States citizen. If you answer yes, they usually let you pass on through."

Now those words sounded good to me.

When we first got in the truck, I was driving and Vinnie was checking out the map. It was already past midnight, but we were finally on our way back to Illinois. When we got to the checkpoint, a police officer came to the window and asked us, "Are you United States citizens?"

We both answered at the same time, "Yes, sir."

So he just motioned us to keep on going. After we drove by, I told Vinnie, "That was pretty easy. Do you want to drive now? I'm feeling a little sleepy."

He said, "Sure."

I was taking a nap when I felt the truck slowing down and moving toward the right. I straightened myself up in the seat and asked him, "What's going on, man?"

He said, "I was speeding a little, and there's a cop pulling us over."

What! We just made it past the checkpoint and you're speeding!" I told him nice and calm, "Just act cool. You have your driver's license on you, right?"

He said, "Yeah."

"Okay, just answer any questions he asks, so we can be on our way."

The policeman got out of his car and walked slowly toward the truck. He asked Vinnie, "Do you have your driver's license with you? I clocked you going eighty."

"I didn't realize I was going that fast sir," Vinnie said.

The policeman told him, "I'll be right back."

I told Vinnie, "Doggone, what in the world were you thinking, man?" Then I added, "That's okay. Just keep talking to him the way you have been."

When the policeman returned, he gave Vinnie his driver's license back. He said, "It's going to be a one hundred dollar-ticket, or you can just post your driver's license until you go to court."

Vinnie said, "I'm not from around here. I'll just pay the hundred dollars."

"I can't take the money right here," You'll have to follow me to the station that's a little up ahead, and I'll give you a receipt there."

We were loaded in the door panels with mota, and we were on our way to the police station so Vinnie could pay his hundred-dollar fine. He went in the station and came out right away. It didn't even take ten minutes, and once again, we were on our way.

I said, "Okay now, when you drive, stay at fifty-five miles an hour. We're not in any kind of a hurry."

Finally, we got home and unloaded the door panels. We took out six square bundles and put them in a large, plastic garbage bag. Then we brought them inside the house, where I opened them up to weigh and check out our load. It was all good, quality stuff, which lasted about a month and a half.

At the perfect time, Hando all of a sudden surprised us when he showed up at the house with a black truck I hadn't ever seen him in before. I thought, *Cool. He got a different four-wheeler.* But then he told me it wasn't his—that it belonged to a young man from the valley. He showed me how it had a really cool secret compartment. A well-hidden, six-inch space ran the length of the bed, between the floor you could see and the one underneath it. It was made especially for smuggling bundles of mota across the checkpoint; in short, it had a second bed built on it. A square hole in the middle was covered by a heavy metal plate, which made it look like a real hitch for one of those big horse trailers. It was held in place by four small, easily removable screws. Once he removed that metal plate, he asked me, "Do you have a wire clothes hanger?

I told him, "Yeah, I'll get you one, and I'll also bring a large, plastic garbage bag." I ran inside the house and went toward the back, where our laundry room was. There, I grabbed the first wire hanger I saw, and as I was going through the kitchen, I picked up a garbage bag. I jumped on the truck and said, "Here you go."

He straightened the hanger, all out except for the round hook part at one end. He put it down into the square hole and started fishing for bundles. When he got done, we had six square-shaped bundles in all, and like usual, it was all high grade Mexican sinsemilla.

The truck didn't look different from any other truck on the road, and Hando showed me that, wherever he jumped on the truck bed, the floor didn't give at all. It felt like the bed of any other truck. I learned that day we shouldn't necessarily always believe what we see or looks can be deceiving.

In this case, I learned, don't always judge a truck by its outward appearance.

We talked as we were unloading the merchandise. Hando said he was tired because he had driven straight through, and he hadn't slept at all. He told me it was about an eighteen-hour drive, so he was going to check into a hotel to get some much-needed rest and we would talk later.

As far as I knew, Hando was a loner. Since the very first time I met him, he was always by himself, which was one of the qualities I liked about him. I've always been able to appreciate a person who's sure of himself and doesn't need to travel with an orchestra, in a manner of speaking.

One of the seven square bundles that I opened up looked like it had a bud from the very top of a plant. It was in the shape of an American bald eagle looking sideways. Or at least that was the first thing that came to my mind when I saw it. Of course, I kept that for my personal stash. That was another load that also lasted about a month and a half.

I kept on going to the convenience store in Pleasant Park, and I would pick up some magazines that had good, quality information on marijuana. Plus, I enjoyed and felt good about seeing close-up pictures of some stuff that looked exactly like what I was selling. I learned that some scientists or a cannabis connoisseur (someone who is well-versed and knowledgeable about marijuana) called a good, quality sinsemilla plant a family member of the *Cannabis sativa* species. It was the crème de la crème—the best of the best; I have also heard it being compared to the champagne of cannabis. On the other hand, I learned about *Cannabis indica*, a lesser quality marijuana species. The high was not as intense, and the buzzed feeling didn't last as long. If we use a wine comparison, *indica* would be like a heavy red selection.

After the month and a half had passed by, I was down to my last quarter pound. But at the perfect time, a car pulled into our driveway that I had not ever seen before. I didn't recognize Hando because he was driving an older model, maroon-colored Buick. It was like he always knew the perfect time to show up. He knew what time I usually got off work, so he didn't ever bother to call before stopping by.

I got a closer look and said, "Hey, Hando. What's up, man?"

He said, "What's up? Do you have a nine-sixteenths wrench and a standard screwdriver?"

"Yeah, I think so."

I took a small toolbox over to him. I thought, *Maybe there's something wrong with the car.*

He scooted the front driver seat forward all the way and folded it down toward the front. He got in the back and told me to bring the tools. He pushed the bottom part of the seat backward so it could get unhooked from underneath and turned it around. I could see a few square-shaped bundles held underneath there with the wires. Then he took the nine-sixteenths wrench and took off four bolts that held the back part of the seat in place. Behind that, in the middle toward the top, was a metal plate held in place by two screws. That's where the screwdriver came in. After he took that off, there was a square hole that we could stick our hand and part of our arm down into, where there were a few more bundles to take out. There was about a six-inch space between the backseat and the trunk area. It had been made especially for carrying bundles of mota. We used that car a couple of times.

The week passed by, and the weekend had finally started. Whenever I wasn't busy with my clients, either dropping something off or picking something up, I liked to go out four wheeling. But I called over to Vinnie and Freddie's first, and told them, "I have to go to Kewanee, and afterward, we can go out to Wawpecong and do a little four wheeling."

They both said, "That sounds like a good idea. Let's go for it, man."

On our way back through Kewanee, we were passing by this car dealership that sold both new and used vehicles. Right up in front and toward the middle, a metallic brown Dodge Ramcharger, with a lift kit and four nice, knobby tires, was on display. I tell you, there's something about that metal flake mixed in with that color; that's what got my head to turn. I really don't think that color by itself would have made me look twice, but the combination of the metal flakes and the color got my curiosity going big-time. I told the guys, "Hey, check out that truck. Let's stop and look at it a little closer."

I pulled into the dealership and parked the Jeep. We all got out and started walking toward the truck. I asked Vinnie and Freddie, "Is this really a truck, because it doesn't have a bed in the back? I've never seen one of these Dodges up close before. I've seen a Ford Bronco and a Chevy Blazer up close. This Dodge is bigger and a little roomier I can see. I think it looks better. Plus, it has carpeting all on the inside."

We were looking through all the windows, and Vinnie said, "Let's see what's under the hood."

I was pleasantly surprised after he opened the hood. It had a big, four-barrel carburetor sitting on a solid, aluminum Edelbrock intake manifold, and it was a high-rise. It also had a nice, big, round chromed air filter. My first thought was, *That combination looks tough and sweet.*

A salesman from the dealership came out and asked us, "Can I help you gentlemen with anything?"

I answered, "Yes, can you tell me about this Dodge?"

The man did his job and told me all about it, and at the end of his sales pitch, he told me how much they were asking for it. He asked me, "Do you have something to trade in for it?"

I said, "Yeah, that Jeep we rode in on, as is. How much are you willing to give me for it?"

He said, "Well, let me take a look at it."

He went back in the dealership and came out with some papers on a clipboard and a pen. After he checked the body, the tires, under the hood, and all around the inside he said, "I'll give you as much as we are asking for the Dodge Ramcharger."

I said, "You got a deal."

After we filled out all the papers, I was the proud owner of a bad-to-the-bone 1979 Dodge Ram. Even though I knew what I had been doing was not cool in God's eyes, a lot of the things I did were pretty decent, "according to the world's way of thinking." The bottom line was, I had been having fun doing things my way, not ever once wanting to hurt anyone on purpose and not ever asking myself, *If I died today, where would I spend eternity?* But if I would have been truthful, my answer would have been hell.

CHAPTER 9

THE OUT-OF-THE-BLUE, BIG BETRAYAL

I was a very happy young man, being a new owner of a Dodge Ramcharger. But I wanted to get something for what I considered my boys, Vinnie and Freddie, to show my appreciation for them always being ready for anything, if I ever called.

One Saturday shortly after I got my Ram, Vinnie and I were cruising around in it. I stopped to get some gas at one of only two gas stations in Pleasant Park. When I pulled in, Vinnie looked up and pointed out a Ford Bronco that had a nice, black paint job, with some yellow, orange, and red flames going back from around its front tire wells. It stood out bold as ever, in the only used car dealership in town, which just so happen to be right by the gas station we pulled into. He was telling me, "Check that truck out, man."

I said, "Yeah, and those flames make it look even cooler. Let's go ask about it."

After I filled my gas tank up and paid, I drove over to the little car dealership. Vinnie and I went in the office area and saw the owner in there. We both knew him and said, "Hey, Bill."

Vinnie asked him, "How much are you asking for the Ford Bronco?"

Bill said, "First of all, it has a solid body with no rust anywhere; a lift kit; and some nice, knobby tires. It's an automatic with a strong 351 V-8 engine, and it has a new paint job; with those flames, you'll be having a lot of girls looking you over." He was sitting at his desk and wrote a number down on a piece of paper and then slid it toward Vinnie. He said, "This is what I can do for you, tax included."

Vinnie picked up the paper and showed it to me. He said, "That looks like a pretty good number to me."

I said, "Get the keys and let's go check it out, man."

Bill reached behind him, opened a cupboard, and grabbed some keys. He handed them over to Vinnie, and we all walked out to the truck. Vinnie got inside the truck and said, "Let's listen to how this bad boy sounds." He turned the truck on and revved it up a couple of times. He said, "That engine sounds nice."

I went around kicking the tires and knocking all around the bottom of the truck's body. I was listening for a thump sound, were Bondo might be trying to hide behind some fresh paint. I walked over close to him and said, "It sounds pretty solid. If you like it, tell him to get the paperwork, and we'll be back with the money."

Vinnie told Bill, "I like it. I'll take it. While you're getting all the paperwork together, me and Johnny will be right back with the money."

We went to my house and came back with the money. The sale only took a few minutes, and in the end, everybody was happy. Bill had more cash than what he'd started out with that day. Vinnie had his first 4x4. And I was able to say, one down and one to go. I told Vinnie, "Follow me over to my house and pick me up so we can go over to Freddie's and you can show him your Bronco."

When we got there, I told Freddie, "Hey man, we need to get you a 4x4. That way, all three of us can have one."

After a couple weeks had gone by, I drove over to Vinnie's and said, "Let's go check out Freddie."

When we got to Freddie's, I said, "Hey, Freddie. What's up, man?"

He said, "Not too much, but when I was driving by Bill's today, I saw he has a light brown Chevy Blazer 4x4 for sale at his place."

"Cool, man. Let's go check out Bill."

As we were getting close to Bill's place, we could see the Blazer Freddie was talking about. From the outside, it looked nice and clean. I told those guys, "Let's go inside and talk to Bill."

As we were walking into Bill's office, he was coming out. We said, "Hey, Bill."

Freddie asked, "What's the deal on that Blazer out there?"

Bill said, "I just got that in. She's nice and clean on the inside and the outside. Let me get you the keys."

Freddie turned her on, and he said, "She purrs like a kitty."

Bill told him all about the Blazer.

I told Freddie, "You and Vinnie, check it out real good, man, and if you like it, it's yours."

After they looked all over the inside, outside, and even under the hood. Then Freddie came over by me and said, "Hey, Johnny, we checked it out real good, and I like it, man."

"Okay. Tell Bill you want it and ask him to figure out how much he needs for it, tax and all and then let you know."

He did and Bill said, "Let's go into my office and talk about it."

Freddie asked him, "Do you have an idea around how much it's going to be? That way, we can go get the money for you real quick."

Bill said, "I'll tell you what; since this is the second vehicle you boys are going to get from me in less than a month, bring me two thousand seven hundred and you can take it."

Freddie, said, "Okay. While you're getting the paperwork ready, we will be right back with the money."

It didn't take us long before we had everything taken care of, and Freddie had his own 4x4 Chevy Blazer. Now all three of us had a 4x4, and I could say, "Mission accomplished." Before Vinnie and Freddie got their 4x4s, they both had cars. But afterward, I didn't ever see them riding in their cars again. So I thought, *Great. They must have liked their four wheelers.*

A few weeks later, at the perfect time, my dad came over and told me, "I saw a car that looked real nice when I was driving back from Kewanee, and I think it would be good for Mary."

I said, "That sounds great, Dad. I have a little money saved up, so I can get Mary a car for her birthday, which is tomorrow. Plus, Christmas is just around the corner. She has put up with so much from me, and she gave me two beautiful children. I think that would be a nice surprise for her. Let's go check that car out, Dad."

As we headed out the door, I yelled upstairs and told Mary, "I'm going with my dad for a little bit, and I'll be back later."

When we got to the dealership, my dad said, "It's that dark maroon car sitting up on top of that ramp thing so everybody can see it."

We climbed the ramp and got close to it. "Hey, Dad," I said, "This looks nice and clean. It says it's a Cutlass Supreme. Who makes that?"

My dad said, "Oldsmobile."

I asked him, "Are Oldsmobiles good cars?"

"Yeah, your Uncle Cisco used to have one, and when he stepped on the gas, it would rock up and down as it was flying down the road."

A man from the dealership came out and asked, "Can I help you gentlemen with anything?"

My dad said, "Yeah, we want to look at this car."

"Well, as you can see, it's nice and clean inside and out. It's an automatic, and the mileage isn't bad. This would make a good family car."

I asked him, "How much are you asking for it?"

He said, "Twenty-nine hundred. Let's go into my office and talk about it."

When all was said and done, I had bought my first Oldsmobile Cutlass Supreme as a combination Christmas and birthday present for my wife. I couldn't see it at the time, but I was just repeating what my dad had done for me the clean and honest way when I was a young boy. He just earned his money solely from the sweat of his brow, while I went about getting mine in a manner that was completely opposite what I'd been taught.

After a few months went by, it was early springtime. Like usual, Hondo didn't call me before showing up. Well, technically speaking, he didn't show up that time. All of a sudden, I just saw a dark-colored truck pulling into our driveway, with two people I had never seen before. I walked out my back door because the man who was driving the truck didn't stop in front. He drove toward the back on one side of the house and parked the truck. We had four dogs, but it's a good thing they were all tied up.

I could see that one of the people in the truck was a woman. As they were getting out of the truck, the man said, "Hando sent you these suitcases."

I said, "Bring them inside. You can just put them in the kitchen."

As soon as my two visitors unloaded several large suitcases, they were gone. I could tell it was all business with those two because, whenever Hando brought me anything, we always had something to talk about while we were unloading the merchandise, and then he would leave. These two didn't even introduce themselves or ask any questions. They just said, "Here are the suitcases we're supposed to give you. Bye."

I took the suitcases from the kitchen and brought them down into the basement in order to check them out better. When I opened the first large suitcase and saw quite a few bundles of mota, I was pleasantly surprised because now I had both quality and quantity at the same time. The way I thought was, *There's only one thing better than quality, and that's a lot of it.*

I had never seen so much quality mota at one time before, but I knew that, if I weighed and bagged it up myself like I usually did, it would take me forever. So I called a couple of good, trustworthy friends I knew from work, Chris and Raul. Chris and Raul always hung out together. I told them, "I need you guys to come over and help me for a few hours."

Chris said, "Sure, Raul and I will be over in a few minutes."

When they got, there I told them, "Come down into the basement with me. I just got this new stuff in, and I need you guys to help me weigh it. I have four boxes of gallon-sized freezer baggies here. I want you to weigh each one of these baggies on the triple beam and, on the left-hand side, write down its weight. Add 112 grams and a sprinkle of shake more or a frog hair more, for a quarter pound. Make me fifty of these. And to the rest, add 224 grams and a frog hair more for half pounds. Before you start, I want you to open up this large, plastic tablecloth underneath the place where you're going to be working. I need you to gently pull the buds apart from off the bundles before you start weighing it. This is good quality stuff, and if there's anything in the bundles that would make it look like anything else, it may need a little help—like you trimming some unnecessary stems off with these clippers, if need be. After you pull a few bundles apart, you should have a decent amount of shake. I want you to clean all the seeds out from it. That's the pile you can use when you need to put a few extra frog hairs in. I want you to make sure that it's always a little bit over."

Chris said, "Sure thing, man."

Raul said, "If that's the way you want it, that's the way you'll get it."

"Thanks, you guys. And if you have any questions, just come upstairs and ask me."

When I got upstairs, the phone rang. It was one of my clients. I said, "Hi, Steve."

He said, "Hi. Can I come over?"

"Sure. I'll see you in a little bit."

After a few minutes passed by, Steve showed up in his car. We had four dogs; three of them were Chow Chows, and the fourth one was a Doberman pinscher. The oldest one was a cinnamon-colored female Chow named Rosie. The second oldest was a black Chow, also a female, named Princess. The third and youngest of our dogs was a male. He was a blue Chow, and his name was Azul (Spanish for "blue"). The Doberman pinscher, who was the third oldest, was a reddish-brown female named Santana. They were all going crazy, barking like they usually did when someone they didn't know pulled into our driveway.

Like normal dogs, they barked a lot. I thought, *That's good. They let me know when someone's here, but enough is enough.* Rosie and Santana where both loose and running around outside. But Azul and Princess were chained up, so I went outside and started yelling at the two that were loose. "Rosie and Santana, don't you dogs remember Steve? Now shut up and get out of here! Don't be scared, man." I told Steve. "They won't bite you. Come on in. Rosie and Santana, you dogs go back to your house, and shut up!" Steve slowly got out of his car, and I said, "You're okay, man. They won't mess with you."

He walked kind of quickly onto our porch and came inside the house, but the dogs kept on barking. I thought, *Maybe there's another dog or something out there getting them all excited.*

I said, "Have a seat, Steve." I opened my client book up, and he took some money out of his pocket and handed it to me. I counted it and told him, "You don't have the entire amount here."

"Yeah, well, I wasn't able to get it all this time," Steve said. "Some of the people didn't pay me."

"That's okay man," I told him. "How much stuff do you think you'll need to take so you can pay me what you owe me and for the stuff you're going to take?"

"I don't know."

I said, "Usually you take a quarter pound and you already know that's two fifty. Do you want a half for five hundred, or can you get rid of a whole pound for nine hundred? If you can sell the pound, it'll be better and cheaper for you; you'll be able to make a lot more money for yourself."

He said, "Okay."

I walked into the kitchen and opened the door that led to the basement and yelled down, "Hey, send me up a pound in a box, man!"

Right away, Raul brought me up a box with a pound in it. I took a quick peek in the box and said, "Here you go, Steve." I asked him what I usually ask all my clients after doing business with them. "Do you want to smoke one?"

"No, I have to go," he said. He seemed kind of nervous and in a hurry to me. I thought it was because he wasn't able to pay me all the money he owed me. As I walked him to the door, I said, "Hey man, everything will be okay. Don't worry. You have a good night and God bless."

The next day, I came home for lunch like usual. I had spoken with Bruno, a client and good friend of mine the night before. We'd agreed to meet at my house at lunchtime because he needed a quarter pound. We took care of everything that we needed to nice and quick, and, wham, bam, thank you, ma'am, we each took off our separate ways.

When I got back to the nursery, it was an afternoon just like every other. At least that's what I thought. I went back to where my crew and I were working at a table, preparing some young cuttings for the upcoming planting season. We were trimming their roots, so I had my clippers in hand. After trimming just a few cuttings, I heard one of only two doors that can be used to get into that part of the building open, and I saw a couple of nicely dressed men walking through the door. At first I thought, *They must be looking for the main office, and they're coming in here to ask for directions.*

To my surprise, when they got close to the table where we were working, they asked for Johnny Zapata. I said, "Yeah, that's me."

One of them said, "Come out here. We need to ask you a few questions."

As I walked toward them from behind the table, one of them took the clippers from out of my hand and a little dagger from out of the sheath I had hooked on my belt. I asked, "Hey, what's going on?"

I guess it was the man in charge of the whole fandango who said, "We just came from your house."

I said, "Okay," with the most relaxed and casual look on my face that I could muster up.

The man that was doing all the talking said, "We found all that stuff in your basement."

"I have a bunch of rocks in there," I replied, maintaining the most serious poker face I have ever tried to display.

"No, that's not what I'm talking about," he answered.

"Well, what are you talking about?" I asked, my eyebrows clinched and my head slightly tilted to the left.

"Oh, you're going to act like you don't know now?" he responded. His voice was a little elevated and aggravation was written all over his face.

"I really don't know what you're talking about," I continued, with a bewildered look on my face, insisting I knew absolutely nothing about what he was talking about.

"Okay, come over here and turn around." After he put the silver bracelets on me, (otherwise known as handcuffs) he patted me down and, at the same time, said those famous words that I'll never forget: "You're under arrest. You have the right to remain silent. Anything you say can and will be used against you in a court of law. You have the right to an attorney, and if you cannot afford an attorney, one will be appointed for you. Do you understand what I just said to you?"

"Yes, sir."

After he escorted me outside, he opened the back door to the squad car, and I got in. The two men both got in the car, and we were on our way to Kewanee. They took me the long way on the back roads. (I think this was done on purpose so that I could see all the other police cars and people at my house on the way to the Kewanee City Police Station.)

When we got to the station, the drug enforcement agent who was driving drove us into the garage and parked the car. He got out and opened my door. They were really nice and decent to me, and they acted like I would expect real professionals to act. I had not ever had my fingerprints or pictures taken for jail purposes before, but I did that day. Then they told me to take my clothes off and put all my belongings into a vanilla envelope and get into an orange jumpsuit.

I asked, "Can I talk to a lawyer and go in front of a judge so I know how much my bond is going to be?"

The head drug agent said, "Yes, I can see to it that you'll go in front of a judge today, if you only cooperate with us and tell us who you get your marijuana from."

"I would, if I knew what you were talking about, but I don't know anything about any marijuana."

"Okay, then you'll have to spend the whole weekend in jail."

"Well I guess I know where I'm going to be this weekend."

The guard who took me upstairs told me, "Everyone is out of their cells on the floor I'm taking you to so they can watch TV, and your cell is on the right-hand side; it's number A-2."

A little later on, another guard brought supper. It's a good thing my mom didn't raise me to be a picky eater because what they brought us to eat didn't exactly look like they had gotten it from Burger King. But I was hungry, so I ate everything. Shortly after that, they told us over the TV speaker it was time to go back to our cells; after praying first, I was able to sleep pretty well that night.

When morning came around, I went to the bathroom and washed my face. Since everything I needed to do that was in the same little area, I was able to get that taken care of pretty quickly.

Shortly after I did that, I was surprised when all the cell doors opened up at once and everybody left their cells and went out to the big open area so we could stretch our legs and watch TV again. We were allowed to stay there for breakfast, lunch, and dinner. I got kind of bored watching so much TV. I was used to washing up and being on the go; whether at work or after work, I was constantly on the move. I hadn't ever been in jail before. This whole thing about being locked up in one room and having food brought to you—that was for the birds. After a while, I even started feeling sorry for the birds. That's no life for anyone.

After breakfast, one of the guards came and told me I had a visitor. He unlocked the cell door and put the silver bracelets on me, then took me into a room where there were a few seats. I saw it was my dad as he took the silver bracelets off me. I sat down across from him, but we were still separated by a thick glass window. He motioned me to pick up the telephone that was on my side. I did, and he asked, "How you doing?"

I said, "I'm doing okay."

"Well, I'm glad. I talked with William, and he told me about a lawyer who is a good friend of his family; he's coming to talk with you a little later on today."

"Okay, that sounds good."

We talked for a few more minutes, and then he said, "I have to go. We will talk later."

I hung the phone up. As the guard put the silver bracelets back on me then took me back from where he had brought me and locked the door behind me. I had to put my hands through a certain part of the cell door so the guard could take the silver bracelets off me. That had to be done anytime I would be going anywhere outside of that area.

That afternoon, a guard came and said my lawyer was downstairs and wanted to talk to me, just like my dad had said. Like always, I knew I could count on my dad to tell me the truth. The guard took me downstairs and put me in a room that had a table and a couple of chairs in it. I saw a man sitting there. He said, "Hi. My name is Jack Mulligan." He shook my hand and added, "I'm going to be representing you. You can call me Jack."

I said, "Hi. My name is Johnny Zapata; you can call me Johnny."

He asked me some questions about what had happened, and I answered them like I remembered they'd happened. He said, "I'll be at the courthouse Monday morning when you get there."

Monday morning came around, and the guard came to get about seven of us. He put handcuffs on our hands in front of us and on our feet and then attached us to a long chain that connected all of us together so we could go to the courthouse, which was across the street from the jailhouse. I'm sure we looked like a bunch of little orange ducklings all in a row on our way over there.

When we got inside the courthouse, the guard took the long chain and our hand and feet cuffs off of us.

I saw Jack and said, "Hi."

He said, "Hi. When we get in there, let me do all the talking, and if the judge asks you something you don't know how to answer, don't say anything. Just look at me, and I'll help you."

When it was my turn to go in front of the judge, he set my bond at $150,000. It was like, wham, bam, thank you, ma'am, real quick. I thought it would take a lot longer than what it did. I found out that I was going to need 10 percent of $150,000, which was $15,000. I had what I needed at the time, and I thank God for my dad.

I told my dad I wasn't going to be messing around with the underground (mota) anymore, because that was a lot of drama that I had put my family through. Starting with my grandma, my mom, my dad, and all my little brothers and sisters, my arrest had affected everyone. Plus Mary and I had two young children at the time; the oldest, Johnny Zapata Jr., and our little girl, Eva Zapata, were both seven years old. Most importantly, I'd hurt my wife. I know the whole family felt bad and it was all my fault.

I gave Jack my telephone number and I had a lawyer calling my house and asking for me, so we could meet after I got out of work. Now that wasn't the way I ever imagined I would meet a lawyer.

I eventually found out Steve was nervous for a good reason the last night he had been over and, that was because he was the one that narcked on me after he had gotten busted himself. I had not ever given him or anyone else a reason to do something like that to me, I always treated everyone like I would like to be treated, and that was decently and with respect. I don't know exactly what the drug agents said to Steve, so he would turn on me, maybe they told him he was going to prison and he was going to be fresh meat in there, "Somebody's Girlfriend," I don't know, but what I do know is that he got scared. I heard the reason for the dogs barking so much that night was, because Steve had the top man from the drug agency in his backseat slouched down. That night to help him out, I was even willing to take a chance and let him take a pound without paying for it first, because I really believed that some of his people had not paid him, so I felt sorry for him.

I learned if you're going to do things the right way in this business and be successful at it; you can't be led by your emotions. In this business, if anyone owes you money the best thing to do is have them pay you first and then talk about getting more merchandise afterwards. Sometimes, you have to be downright ruthless and not really care about anybody else. Anyone who knew the real me knew that was just not like me; that was before this incident happened.

Slowly but surely, my callous began to get a thicker lining of skin on it, in a manner of speaking. So my ways of acting, thinking, and speaking began to change big-time. I really felt betrayed. It felt like someone had stuck a dagger in my back and twisted it all around inside me, and I didn't have the slightest idea it was coming.

When I got back to our house, I was looking all around to see what kind of damage had been done during the drug raid. The first place I looked was in the dining room, where I had a gun cabinet because I had a small collection of guns. I had a gun that looked like a Tommy gun, like back in the olden days, except I didn't have a round clip for it. It had a straight clip; that one was a .45 caliber. I also had a brand spanking new Mini-14 that I had bought at a local K's Merchandise store. It had a pistol grip and a folding stock, and it looked real nice. That one was a .223 caliber. Last but not least where my rifles are concerned was a .30-caliber M1 carbine from the Korean era that was in really good condition. I had a TEC-9 that came with an extra clip, two extra barrels, and a suppressor that looked exactly like a silencer, all three of which I could screw on the end of the barrel. It all came in an attaché case with combination locks on both sides. I called that one my street sweeper. I also had two handguns; one was a 380 Smith and Wesson, and the other one was a .32 Walther PPK that had a German stamp on it, that one alone was valued at $500. I didn't ever use them for anything illegal. I just liked target shooting with them, and the DEA took every single one of them.

The gun cabinet had two small doors on the bottom where I had a whole bunch of rounds of ammunition for all my guns. Just about all of them I had gradually bought at a local gun show; they didn't take the ammunition, but like I said they did take all my guns. That was also where I kept an old makeup case that I used to put money in from my second job, and they didn't miss that either. I checked on top of the gun cabinet and found a glass frame that had a sparkly red, green, and gold picture that said *Cannabis sativa and Cannabis indica* and had marijuana leaves all over it, which I used to cut up cocaine on. I said, "Wow, man. They missed this." I went and checked on the top of the refrigerator, and in a plastic container, I had a piece of a special looking marijuana bud with some shake and rolling papers that was my stash at the time, which they also missed. I took a quick peek downstairs in the basement, and yeah, they had cleaned that out pretty well; they didn't miss anything down there.

As I was passing through the living room, I told my wife, "Let's go upstairs and take a look in our bedroom." Once there, I asked her, "What in the world happened to the little door that was at the bottom of my filing cabinet?" I could see the side where the lock was had gotten all bent up where they had pried it open. She told me the drug agents had made her all nervous because the door on the filing cabinet was locked and they wanted her to hurry up and give them the key. At the time, she couldn't remember where it was. I said, "My goodness. I didn't even have anything in there. They didn't have to pry it open like that. You should have given them the key."

Again she said, "I got so nervous, I couldn't even begin to remember where the key was."

I said, "That's all right. They probably thought I had something else in there they could charge me with."

A little after five o'clock rolled around, I told my wife, "Let's go over to my mom and dad's house, but before we get in the car, let me grab that plastic container with the weed in it from off the top of the refrigerator, along with the frame with the marijuana leaves on it."

After we all got in the car and I reached the end of the short lane that was our driveway, I got out of the car and took that frame with the marijuana leaves on it and threw it in the burning barrel. It broke in pieces.

When we got about halfway to my mom and dad's house, we were at the top of a hill. I pulled the car over and stopped, grabbed the little plastic container I had underneath my seat, and opened the car door. I inconspicuously looked to the right and to the left and then walked across the road, opened the container, and dumped everything that was in there in the weeds. I closed the container as I got back in the car and continued to my mom and dad's house.

Once we got there, we all got out and went inside the house. I told my mom, dad, and grandma, "When I got home, I went around looking through the whole house to see what kind of damage had been done when they were going through the house, and it didn't look bad."

My grandma said, "After they all left, your mom and I went over to your house, and you should have seen how it looked. Everything was thrown on the floor. It was terrible. It looked like a tornado had gone through there. But me and your mom straightened it out and put things back in their place."

"Thanks. They didn't find a little container that I had on top of the refrigerator with a little bit of marijuana that I used for myself."

My dad said, "Don't be messing around with that stuff anymore."

"No, Dad. I stopped on top of the hill when we were coming over here, and I threw it all away."

"Good ... Your mom, grandma, and Mary can't be dealing with all this mess. You're going to kill them."

"I know, Dad. That's not good, and I'm going to stop messing around with that stuff."

It says in the Bible, "As a dog returns to his own vomit, so a fool repeats his folly" (Proverbs 26:11 NKJV). I found out that old habits are hard to break, especially if we try to break them all on our own. I was able to stay clean for a week, but after the week went by, I was looking on the hill where I had dumped all the mota that was in the little, plastic container and found nothing.

I started talking and hanging around with some of my old friends; they would offer me some of their weed that they had to smoke, and I did notice quite a difference.

They said, "It's nothing like the weed you used to get."

I said, "I know. It takes a lot more of this stuff to get me to the place where I want to be, and that's nice and mellowed out."

One day after work, I was at home and the phone rang. I instantly recognized the voice on the other end. It was Hando. He said, "What's up? How have you been doing?"

I said, "I've been doing pretty good, besides not being able to find anything around town like the weed you used to bring me. I think it's because I'm used to that good, quality stuff."

"If you want, I will give you this guy's number; he's keeping some mota for me, and he only lives a little distance away from you. It's about an hour away in Indiana."

"Yeah, that would be great."

After I talked with a few of my older and more trustworthy clients, I guesstimated that I was going to need at least five pounds; that would hold me over for a couple of weeks. I wanted to feel my way around things and start out slowly. I called the number Hando gave me and found out I had heard about this guy before. He was known as TJ. I told him in Spanish, "I need to work on my truck, but I need five special wrenches. Do you have any tools I can use?"

He said, "I sure do. I can help you out with that." That sounded like music to my ears.

After he told me how to get to his house, I told him, "I'll meet you there at seven thirty after the sun goes down and it's a little dark."

When I got there, he was sitting in his car and told me to follow him. He took me down this secluded, old country road, a place where we could see quite a distance in front of us and behind us. I pulled up right beside him. He got out of his car and opened his trunk. As I quickly did the same, I said, "Hey, TJ, what's up!"

He said, "What's up!"

We put what he had in his trunk in mine, and I said, "I'll see you later."

He said, "Yeah." And wham, bam, thank you, ma'am, we were off our separate ways.

As I was driving down the road to go back home to Illinois, I was listening to the radio and what was playing was, "Back in Black."

The next day was a Friday. After I got off work and finished doing all the things I usually did, I called up Vinnie. He answered, and I said, "Hey, what's going on, man?"

He said, "Not too much."

"I'll be over in a few minutes so we can go for a cruise."

"All right, I'll be waiting."

Once I got to his house, I asked, "Are you ready to go for a cruise?"

He said, "Yeah, but let's go check out Jacob at his mother's house first." Jacob was another partying friend of ours. Jacob lived at his mom's house in Kewanee. Vinnie had already talked with him on the phone, and he said that Jamie, another mutual friend of ours, was there with him and wanted to go cruising around with us.

When we got to Jacob's mom's house, I honked, and both of them ran out. Vinnie bent his seat forward to let them get in the backseat of the Ram. I said, "Get in, you guys."

Vinnie asked, "Are you ready to party?! Do any of you have any smoke on you?"

Jamie said, "I got some super fresh quaaludes. They're lemon 714s, double *M* on the word *lemon*, so fresh you can see a little extra ring around the middle edge where they've been pressed together."

Jacob said, "Stop by the liquor store. I have five bucks. Come on, you guys; cough up some money, so we have at least a case to start the night out with."

Between the four of us, we easily got enough for a case.

I said, "I don't have any mota with me right now, but let me check out one of those quaaludes. I've never tried one of these before, so what is this supposed to do for me?"

Jamie said, "This is a heavy-duty downer; it'll relax you real good."

I said, "I'm not feeling hyper or like jumping around uncontrollably. I don't really need to be relaxed. I've tried speed before but never a downer.

Let me check one of those out. Pass me a beer from back there so I can wash this down with."

Jacob said, "Here you go, man."

I said, "Thanks. I've tried pink ladies, yellow jackets, black beauties, white crosses, all different kinds of speed, but never any kind of a downer before. To be honest with you guys, I haven't even heard of a quaalude before."

I was about to receive a Missouri Mule kick, but way down low instead of up. I'm glad I didn't decide to try two of those at once. They looked like pregnant aspirins to me, with the word *lemmon* on the top outer edge and the number 714 right underneath it in the middle of the tablet. We were driving down East Oak Street in Kewanee, and it was eleven o'clock at night.

About twenty-five minutes after we had all taken a quaalude, all of a sudden, *BAM!* Out of nowhere I just fell asleep at the wheel while driving. That had not ever happened to me before. Quite a few cars were parked on the right side of the street, and though fewer were on the left, cars were parked sporadically along the entire street on that side as well.

When I fell asleep, my left hand pulled the steering wheel down. I ended up where there was a gap and no cars or trees, as my right hand slid straight down the right side of the steering wheel. When I hit the six-inch high cement lip on the left side of the street, my right foot, which was on the gas pedal, pushed it all the way down. When I suddenly woke up, my right arm flew up and hit the gear shifter past neutral and into reverse. I was burning rubber on the street in reverse and slammed the brakes on when I was in the middle of someone's front yard. I tried to shift it into drive so we could get out of Dodge, but with all the commotion going on, the man whose yard I was on came out of his house pretty quickly, along with some of his surrounding neighbors.

He started yelling and pointing at me, "Stop. Stop. He's trying to drive away!"

After several attempts of trying to put the truck in drive, I realized that, for some reason, I couldn't move the shifter or turn the steering wheel, so I just turned the truck off, opened my door, and told the man, "I was just trying to get the truck off your yard."

With all the neck jerking and the smell of burnt rubber from the tires and the whole ordeal, unsurprisingly, all four of us in my vehicle, at the same time, got completely sober. I don't know exactly who it was, but someone quickly called the police. It didn't take the responding officer long at all, and he was right there.

Before the policeman got close to us, I told the guys, "Just follow my lead and agree with everything I say."

He came up to me and asked, "Were you driving?" I said, "Yes."

"Tell me what happened."

"There was a dark-colored car coming the opposite way, and it was moving pretty fast, so I didn't get a chance to see the person driving. I had to swerve to the left to avoid hitting the other car. It's a good thing there wasn't a car parked there or a big tree. When I hit the lip on the edge of the street my right hand flew up and hit the gear shifter in reverse and I ended up in this man's front yard. It all happened so fast, I don't know if my truck got hit or scratched on the right side when the other car went by me. Let me take a quick look."

Those guys just looked at me with their eyes bugged out. I don't know if that was because they were a little bit in shock, but that made my story look even more believable. Maybe they were surprised at how fast I made up the story when I was talking to the policeman and the serious look I had on my face. The policeman said, "I need to talk to the man whose property this is. I'll be right back."

When he came back, he said, "I have all the information for my report. I called Petersons Towing to come get your truck, and if you need a ride anywhere, I can take you."

Now let me break this one down to you. That night when we went to pick up Jacob and Jamie so they could come cruising around with us, Jamie already had the quaaludes. So when the perfect amount of time had passed by after we took the quaaludes, I fell asleep at the wheel exactly at the right time for my left hand to pull down on the steering wheel, so the truck was at the precise angle we needed to be at. Only God knew when that happened there wasn't going to be a car or tree where I went over to the left and hit the street cement lip. When that happened is when my right foot pushed the pedal all the way down to the metal. Then my right hand that had slipped down off the steering wheel flew up against the gear shifter and knocked it into reverse. The combination of the sudden impact of my left front tire with the street cement lip, and my right arm flying up against the gear shifter caused a piece in my gearbox to break, disabling the steering wheel to be moved so the angle that we hit the street lip going forward was the precise angle we needed while burning rubber backwards at a high rate of speed to miss all the parked cars, and we ended up safely in a man's front yard. When I told the policeman the story of what supposedly happened; God didn't give me a blank mind. It was a good thing the policeman didn't search the truck, instead he called Petersons towing to take the truck away.

It just so happened that the owner of Petersons Towing was a client of mine. On Monday morning, I called him and he told me, "The boys found the opened case of beer that was in the back of your truck and they got rid of it for you."

I said, "Thanks."

Once again, never fear, for God is always here.

CHAPTER 10

IF GOD BE FOR ME, WHO CAN BE AGAINST ME

It looked like any other late summer Friday night, but by no means was it going to be a regular one. I had gone over to Jan and Danny's house as I was accustomed to, especially on a Friday night. But this night out of all the regulars, only Robbie had come over

When Danny all of a sudden said, "Hey, Johnny, do you want to go to a party, man?" I said, "Yeah, that sounds like a fun time, man. Hey, Robbie, you want to come with us?"

"Yeah, let's go check it out, man. Where is this party supposed to be at anyway?"

Danny said, "It's over in Wilsonville."

I said, "Let's go party, man."

Danny told Jan, "We're going over to Wilsonville. We'll be back later."

When we got there, we immediately targeted the keg of beer, paid a dollar, and got our cups. Quite a few people were there, but we didn't really know anybody, so we drank slowly, talked, and mainly stayed to ourselves.

After a few hours had gone by and we for sure had drunk our dollars' worth of beer, Danny said, "Hey, you guys, why don't we get out of here, man?"

I said, "Yeah, come on, Robbie."

As we were headed out the door and went by the coatracks, I asked Danny, "Can you grab my green coat from there?"

He asked, "Which one, this one?"

I said, "Yeah."

Danny grabbed it, and we all walked out the door. When we were walking out to the truck, he said, "I didn't remember you having a coat."

I told him, "I didn't. I just liked the way that one looked. Thanks, man."

Danny said, "If the owner of the coat would have seen me, I could have gotten my butt beat."

We all started laughing as we got closer to the truck. That's when I took the coat from him and put it on. I said, "It fits pretty good. Let me check the pockets and see if I have anything in here."

As I drove us back to Danny's house, I told him again, "Thanks for the coat. It fits me just right."

Robbie said, "I was thinking, *I don't remember seeing Johnny with a coat.*"

I said, "Thanks to Danny, I've got a pretty good-looking army trench coat now." We all laughed again.

Stealing was not something I usually did, but I thought it would be kind of challenging, just to see if I could get away with it, and I did.

When we finally got to Danny's house, I told the guys, "Hey, I'm kind of tired. I'm going to head home. I'll see you guys tomorrow, man."

Two days later, when Monday morning came around and I was at work, I thought, *All right, I got to see another Monday.* Noontime finally rolled around. As usual, everybody who was out in the fields came back to the building where we had clocked in for a half-hour break. We had the option of either staying there and enjoying the whole half hour or going wherever we wanted, as long as we were back by twelve thirty.

As usual, my two cousins, Miguel and Pedro, (they were known as Mike and Pete) were waiting for me at my truck. I usually went home to eat and smoke a couple of bongs full of mota before I came back to work. They liked smoking mota too. Plus, we always had good conversations. That whole day, even up to that time, seemed pretty normal. We all got in the truck, and I started driving to my house. About half a mile away from the nursery, at a place where I had driven many times before, there's a curve on the way to my house. I was driving at a normal speed, but for some reason that day, my truck started sliding sideways.

When it finally came to a stop, I said, "Whoa, is everybody okay?"

I don't know if there was something on the road that made it extra slick or what. The truck ended up with part of its body in the other lane and the front part of the truck down even farther toward the bottom off the road. I put it in reverse and straightened it out in order to continue home. My cousin Mike said, "I just about got killed with one of these big rocks you have back here."

As we all laughed, I said, "As long as no rocks got broken, it's okay."

I have always liked collecting rocks of all sizes. One of the reasons I liked working at the nursery was that we had to switch from place to place, depending on the trees or shrubs that were needed, and that would give me a chance to look in different places for all kinds of rocks.

It was a good thing no car was in the opposite lane—especially when the truck was sliding sideways on the curve—or it could have been bad news. I thank God for small miracles.

Finally, after so many years of me messing around with the underground, I started seeing what I had—a beautiful wife who had given me two precious children. I didn't understand and I couldn't explain it at the time, but I felt a deep desire to spend more time with them. So on the weekends, I wouldn't schedule anything that would take me away from them—not even going out four wheeling, and I really enjoyed doing that.

I had some money saved up so I could do something for our children. So I took my wife and the children to one of the nearby stores and looked at a few different swing sets. I picked the one I thought they could have the most fun on. It had a slide, two regular swings, and a Kettler glider swing that had space for one or two little people to sit opposite each other and then push with their feet and pull on the pole in front of them. It also had a little trapeze, and the last piece was called a gondola swing. It had space on it for up to four little people to sit, two on each side sitting opposite each other and pushing with their feet, while hanging on to a pole on their right or left side, depending on where they were sitting. In 1985, that wasn't a bad swing set to have.

But putting it together was a whole ordeal all on its own. I wanted our children to get to play on it as soon as possible. So I took on the task of putting it together by myself. I thought, *How hard can this be? It's just a swing set. I'll be able to have this put together in a few easy hours.*

After starting on it, I would soon find out there were some holes that needed to be lined up in order for a bolt to go through them. Since I was dealing with metal, I will have to admit, it didn't bend too easily. So I did let my peace get stolen. I started talking to an inanimate object; shortly after that. I started yelling at it. Then I started to yell out cuss words, about as fast as a Gatling gun spits out bullets. The bad thing about that was, it wasn't the first time I used cuss words. As a matter of fact, I used them just about all the time every day. I noticed I had been getting worse; as time went by, I even made up new ones that I hadn't ever heard of before.

Eventually, I finished putting the swing set together all by myself because who would want to be around a person that was cussing up a storm? I can't think of too many people. My wife and children already knew what kind of a person I was. So they would just stay away from me if I was in one of my cussing frenzies.

After I eventually calmed myself down, because I had finished with the swing set, I called the children and told them to come try out their new swing set. I think that, in part, as I was letting out that string of colorful words, I was tapping into my frustration and anger at Steve for narking on me without a cause.

Usually on Saturdays, especially if I didn't have to go to work on that day, I would try to get up at a decent time. For me that was between seven thirty and eight in the morning. I would use the Weed Eater first and then cut the grass, while my wife pulled weeds out from between her flowers. Since we had a nice-sized front yard, along with the sides and the back, it would take me a few hours to finish with everything. But every time after finishing, I would get a great sense of accomplishment.

I would usually fire up the grill after that. Depending on what we had in the refrigerator, I might throw on some chicken, hotdogs, or hamburgers. Out of foil, I even made a rectangle-shaped container a couple different times. That way, I could cook some fish in butter and squeeze some lemon juice on top. (That's what I'm talking about; shut the door, shut the door.)

For the first time ever, I really started getting into fishing. On the nursery property, there was a stocked pond where I had gotten permission to go fishing. After finishing with whatever we had to do at home on the weekends, I would load up our three fishing rods and the tackle box. My wife went fishing with us one time, and she did a lot of murmuring and complaining about how the fish stunk. She didn't ever go fishing with us again. That didn't discourage the children or me from going fishing just about every weekend, weather permitting.

At first, it would just be the three of us. Then one Saturday I drove little Eva and Johnny Jr. over to my mom and dad's house. After we visited a little, I asked my mom "Is it okay with you if I ask Ramiro and Ruben if they want to go fishing with us?" Ramiro and Ruben were my little brothers.

"Yeah," my mom said. "You just have to keep a close eye on them real good, especially Ruben." Ruben was a few months older than my son. "Make sure they don't get too close to the water's edge," my mom continued, "because they could fall in."

I didn't know exactly what she was thinking because, when you go fishing, you have to get close to the water. That's part of the fun, along with every once in a while putting your hands in the water to clean them. But if you can see the fish in the water when they're nibbling on your worm, you get even more excited and want to get closer.

We would catch some little bluegills from off a deck that was there. After a while, we saw some bigger bluegills that came close to our worm-covered hooks and started nibbling on them. I heard that the nursery had stocked the pond with small bluegills, which we caught plenty of. They'd also put in some small and largemouth bass. (Now those we hadn't seen any of yet.)

After a couple of weeks passed by, I started watching some fishing shows on TV, and I was introduced to the trouble hook and fishing with a lure. After I saw that, I bought some lures that had feathers covering up a treble hook. We were all pleasantly surprised when we saw bass really went for that.

I even got to see some lures that looked like little minnows. I could see how the fish would go for that, but there were others like I mentioned before that simply looked like a bunch of different-colored feathers all tied together. Most of them were accompanied by treble hooks. To my amazement, the bass really went after those. The part I really liked about using lures was that I didn't have to go looking for worms and then put them on the hook, cast out, and wait. Instead, I would cast out and reel it back in over and over again.

One of the times I did that, I was pleasantly surprised to feel a strong tug and see that my lure had disappeared down into the water, just like I had seen on TV. I started reeling in my fishing line, and on the far end, I saw a really nice-sized largemouth bass. I will never forget that day. I had absolutely no idea how good I could feel simply by doing more family type things like going fishing.

I started to think, *Without a doubt, I don't know exactly what's going to happen. But what I do know is that I'm not going to prison.* Without knowing it, I was prophesying my future. All of those little adventures put together that I had gone through were only to prepare me for what I was heading for—the valley of the shadow of death. I wouldn't be alone because Almighty God said in His word, "I will never leave you nor forsake you" (Hebrews 13:5, NKJV).

I started to think, *I'm twenty-four years old, and I've been at this second job since I was sixteen. I think it's about time for me to start growing up and act my age, not my shoe size.* I knew that, over the years, I had seen a lot of money pass through my hands. So I told myself, *I want to get out of this business, but before I do, I want to leave with $100,000 cash profit.*

I knew it would probably take me a few years, but I also knew that, if I had done it before, I could do it again. Finally I had a goal; I really liked spending time with my family instead of spending my time messing around with the underground.

In the meanwhile, it was back to business as usual. Everything seemed to be moving smooth as silk. After a few months passed by, December came around once again. It seemed like one more new year was almost here. Like all the other years, on the twenty-fourth of December, we got together at my mom and dad's house to open presents. We ate a lot of good food with dessert afterward, while drinking pop, joking around, and just having a good old time with the family. After we had spent almost the whole day there, and the torn-up wrapping paper, along with the bows, had all gotten thrown away in a few large garbage bags, it was time for me to take my family back to our house. But before I went outside and started carrying presents to the truck, I asked my dad, "Hey, Dad, what are you going to do after this?"

He said, "I'm going to the bar."

"I'll see you there after a little bit," I told him. "I'm just going to take the family home."

It was the twenty-fourth of December, Christmas Eve, so my wife naturally wanted me to stay at home with her and the children. But I had already told my dad I would see him at the bar. My mind was already made up, and that was it.

After I dropped my family off at our house, I told my wife, "I'm going to check out my dad. I'll see you later, babe. I'm going to take your car."

I drove over to Lucinda's. I didn't see my dad's truck in the parking lot, but I still parked the car and went inside. I asked her, "Hey, Lucinda, has my dad been here tonight?"

She said, "No."

"Okay, thanks." I turned around and didn't even sit down for a drink or anything; I just went back out the door and to the car. I felt a strong desire I hadn't ever felt before to find my dad and, for some reason, just spend more time with him that night. I think I have somewhat of an idea of what an unsuspecting moth feels like when it sees the light from a campfire. I felt like a man on a mission. I had told my dad I would see him in a little bit, and my little bit was running out. I drove south from Lucinda's for a few miles. As soon as I had crossed somc railroad tracks, I was in the little town of St. Austin; where Mary used to live with her mom, sister, brother-in-law, and their family before I asked her to marry me.

The town wasn't very big, but it had three bars. The one where quite a few of us from the nursery had started going to was named Al Oeste, Spanish for "To The West". My guess was the name came from the bar's location; as you headed south into town, if you turned to the right, you'd find the bar on the west side of town. We knew the man who had just opened that bar. He used to work at the nursery with us, so we considered him a friend. Everybody knew him by his nickname, El Toro "The Bull". I saw my dad's truck parked outside. I thought, *Cool, my dad's here, and I don't have to go looking for him anywhere else.*

When I finally went in, it was around six o'clock in the evening. As I got out of my car, I saw ice and snow in the parking lot. Wherever I stepped, I could hear the snow crunching as I compacted it down with each step I took. When I got inside, I said hi to El Toro. He was behind the bar, and I told him, "Give me a Jack and Coke." As I was sitting on one of the stools at the bar I asked him, "Where's my dad?"

He said, "He's toward the back."

"Oh, that's cool. What's he drinking? I want to buy him a drink."

"Okay, I'll take it over to him right now."

I went over to where my dad was, and all night we had good, mellow conversation. We had a good time, and before we knew it, it was already closing time. We had no idea that was going to be the last time we would ever have a drink together there. We both knew and were good friends with El Toro, so when he said, "Last call," while some people started to leave right away, we and a few others, said, "Bring me one more for the road."

Two guys (Raul and Miguel) who I knew came up to me and asked, "Can you give us a ride home?"

"Sure, just let me finish this drink."

After a few short minutes, both my dad and I were done. We all said, "We'll see you later, Toro."

Outside, we could see our breath as we were walking to our vehicles. I took my keys out of my pocket and unlocked my door. I opened it and pushed the power door lock button to unlock the other doors. Raul got in the front, and Miguel climbed in the back. I turned the car on and let it run for a few minutes. I looked in my rear view mirrors and then took a quick peek on both sides. I put it in reverse and turned my steering wheel to the right as I was moving backwards. Then, shifting into drive, I drove for a little ways. When I got to the stop sign, I turned left on Route 10 and headed north out of town.

We hadn't made it too far from the tracks, about a mile, when a man who was at the bar with us and who I considered a friend (and still do), passed us on the left in his car and hit the left corner of my back bumper with the right corner of his front bumper. Now slowly, try to picture this in your mind. The right front corner of his bumper gave the kiss of death to the left back corner of my bumper. That caused my car to start sliding sideways on the road, while at the same time, going down into the frozen ditch on my right side. When my car made contact with the ditch, I hit my mouth on the steering wheel. That's when I broke my two top front teeth and loosened my four front bottom teeth dramatically.

At the same time, my hands slipped off the steering wheel and my knuckles hit the dashboard. That's when they got all cut up. With the speed and momentum we had going when we hit the frozen ditch, the car started flipping the hard way—back bumper over the front bumper—about three times. Because it was at a slight angle when we initially hit the ditch and I didn't have my seatbelt on, my body flew toward my side window. The left front side of my head broke the window, and I continued with that motion. That's when I hit the steel top part of the door, a piece of my skull broke in and was pushing down on my brain making it bleed. About half of the skin on my head and hair got torn back. It was like I had gotten scalped but only on half of my head.

I thank God I always wore a small, black, leather hat at that time. I believe that's what helped me so I wouldn't get cut up by the glass as badly as I could have. I also thank God I was thrown out during the first flip; and landed a little distance away from where the car ended up, because my side was crunched down the most. I would have been smashed like a cockroach.

My dad had decided to take the back way home. While all this was going on, something or maybe I should say Someone got his attention and had him look over toward the right and up into the sky. He saw some lights, which unbeknownst to him, were the lights from my car when it was flipping around. He thought to himself, *Johnny was going home that way.* So he decided when he got to his stop sign instead of turning to the left to go home, he'd turn right in order to get on Route 10 and head north.

He didn't know it at first, but he drove right by where the accident had just happened. He drove all the way up by Lucinda's and turned around. He was driving south toward St. Austin again, and only God knows why, but he was able to see that an accident had just happened. So he stopped and ran out to a previously harvested frozen cornfield, where the car and I had ended up at. He was startled because he didn't see me in the car or anywhere. He asked the man who was in the passenger side, "Where's Johnny?"

But both of the men must have been in shock because they were just looking straight forward, unable to talk. Beto anxiously started looking all around. Some distance away from the car, he could make out something. He made his way over there as quickly as possible. To his surprise, he found my body in a puddle of blood. I was gasping for air, and blood was coming out of my mouth and nose. It was super cold; the ground was frozen solid, and there was snow all over the place. He tried to keep my head from touching the cold, hard, snow-covered ground. He called for the other man who was with him, a man named Salomon. He told him to bring the pancho that he always carried with him in the truck so he could cover me up. To this day, I truly believe this also was God orchestrated; the accident happened at a spot between a house that stood by itself and a small subdivision. So someone who had seen or heard the crash must have called 9-1-1. Before Salomon could bring the pancho to him, a police officer from St. Austin pulled up with a blanket and ran over to where my dad was.

Shortly after they'd covered me up, an ambulance arrived. The EMTs hurried and brought the stretcher out to where I was lying in a puddle of blood. After putting a neck brace on me, they put me on the stretcher and strapped me down. My dad helped them push the stretcher through the snow to the ambulance. They loaded me up and took me to Mercy Hospital in Kewanee.

My dad took Salomon back to where he was staying and rushed over to the emergency room of Mercy Hospital. He told the nurses he was my dad, and they told him to have a seat because, at that moment, the doctors were working on me. After some time had passed by without any word, a nurse finally came to the emergency room and said, "Mr. Zapata, if there's anybody you need to call to come see Johnny, you better call them. I'm sorry. He's dead."

After the nurse left the room, my dad went to one of the corners and knelt down to pray. After he'd had a heart-to-heart talk with God Almighty, he felt a peace come over him, like God was telling him He had everything under control and all was well. So my dad got up and went back to the chair where he was sitting.

A few minutes later, the same nurse came back to the emergency room and said, "Johnny is alive again! Once we're able to stabilize him, we'll move him up north to Mount Calvary Hospital in Terryville. They're better equipped to handle what he needs."

My dad said, "Okay." He went and used one of the phones on the wall to call his house. My mom answered and asked, "How is Johnny doing?"

After telling her I was okay, he asked to talk with my brother, Roman, because he was the only one with a license who could drive at that time. He told Roman, "Go pick up Mary and the children. Leave the children with your mom and grandma at the house. Bring Mary to the emergency room at Mercy Hospital."

Roman said, "Okay. How is Johnny doing?"

My dad responded, "He's doing fine. Just hurry up because they're going to move him up north to Mount Calvary Hospital in Terryville."

My brother had a Camaro Z28. He already had his clothes on, so he just put his coat on and was off. He did what my dad told him. When they were getting close to the hospital, Roman and Mary could see that I was quickly getting loaded up, and we were headed toward Mount Calvary Hospital in Terryville. My brother tried to catch up with the ambulance in his Z28, but his efforts were in vain.

When they finally got to the emergency room of Mount Calvary Hospital, the people Mary spoke with in the ER didn't ask her how her trip was or if she wanted something to drink. They didn't even tell her to have a seat and they would keep her updated. What they did ask her was whether she would like to donate my organs. Now that is no question a wife of eight years should have to answer about her husband. They kept asking her and asking her, and finally she just told them they needed to ask her father-in-law. My guess is they thought I was out for the count, and they wanted to get my organs as fresh as possible.

There is a time and place for everything. But I really don't think that was the time or the place for that question.

To a lot of people's surprise, I was put in the ICU ward instead of a morgue. I was on a bed that would slowly twist me to the left and to the right, which was intended to prevent me from getting pressure sores. I wasn't able to talk in full sentences because my left lung had gotten a hole in it and had collapsed. I had also broken my left clavicle. That's a fancy medical word for a collarbone. In addition, I'd shattered my fifth vertebrae —again that's a fancy medical word for a backbone.

I was very limited when it came to talking because of the collapsed lung, but I was trying to get Mary to understand that I felt very uncomfortable. I wasn't able to pinpoint the exact spot. I was telling her that, somewhere at the very bottom of my spine I was hurting. I told the nurses that a couple of times. But because I wasn't able to communicate normally, frustration was starting to get the best of me.

When Mary told one of the nurses that I was feeling uncomfortable around my lower back, the nurse told her, "Because of his injury, it's impossible for him to feel that area. He must be experiencing phantom feeling." In other words, she believed the pain was all in my head.

No one told me at the time, but the nurse told my family that I would never feel or move anything from my shoulders down ever again.

The next day, when my dad and wife came to see me, one of the nurses told them they had put some gauze and medicine on my tailbone area because I had gotten a skin breakdown. Mary said, "I told you yesterday that he said he felt pain somewhere on his lower back, but you said he was just having phantom feeling."

I was there at that hospital for a total of two months. The doctors had me on some heavy-duty pain medicine. It was a combination of morphine and Valium. I remember absolutely no pain.

Then I was moved to a rehab hospital that was next door. It was called the Rehabilitation Institute of Terryville, or the RIT for short. I was there for three months. So it was five months total up north in Terryville for me. Before that, I had been in the hospital one time for walking pneumonia, and I was there for a total of two days.

Initially when I was moved to the RIT, my rehabilitation team started sitting me up in a motorized power chair, and they also started weaning me off some of the pain pills. Once I started knowing more about my surroundings and my head didn't feel like it was in the clouds, I felt better. At first, I didn't know what day, month, or even year it was.

I had to go talk to a psychologist, and every day, he would ask me the same questions. If I knew who the president or the vice president were, what day it was, and what the month and the year were. Initially, I couldn't remember the answers to any of those questions. Then one morning when they sat me up in my power chair, I paid closer attention to the wall kitty corner from me. Of my three roommates, one had a giant calendar on his wall. From then on, every morning, I would always take a look at his calendar before leaving the room. It was so big a blind person could see the year and month. Another thing that helped was every morning, whoever was his nurse's aide that day would cross out the day before. I went about three more times to go see the psychologist after that day, and then I didn't have to go anymore.

I also had to go to the physical therapy, or PT department. Sometimes, the physical therapists would come to us on our floor and give us therapy in the TV area. One time when they were testing my senses, they determined that I would never feel or move anything from my solar plexus down. That's another fancy way of saying from the top of my stomach down.

One Friday afternoon, a couple of months into my rehabilitation, one of the nurses told me I had a visitor. It was an unexpected surprise for me, the head drug enforcement agent. I said, "Mike, what are you doing here?"

He said, "I had to come up to Terryville and take care of some business. So I thought, *Let me stop by and check out Johnny at the RIT.*"

"Thanks for stopping by," I said.

"You're looking good. How have you been feeling?"

"Better, thanks for asking."

"I have some good news for you," he said.

"Oh yeah; I could use some good news." I answered him, as I was sitting on my battery-operated wheelchair.

"Your case was thrown out of court, but I'm going to keep your guns. You can't use them anyways."

"I have some relatives that can use them," I said.

"No, but, hey, I have to go. You take care."

This one was a biggie, let me break this one down to you the best that I can. In the spring of 1985, when I initially stopped messing around with the drugs, thanks to the DEA. That only lasted about one week, and then I was at it again. In my mind everything seemed to be back to normal for me. I thought *the only thing I need to do is be more careful and it will be okay with God,* that was my way of justifying my actions. After getting busted with 114 pounds of real good high-grade quality weed in my basement, not counting the one that Steve had, any normal person would have gone to prison for a number of years. I didn't know how it was going to happen, but all I knew is without a doubt I was not going to prison; I had absolutely no idea I would be in a wheelchair for over thirty-eight years though. After the car accident happened God allowed me to see, I could be as careful as possible, but I still had no control over anybody else's driving. In conclusion, every single thing that happened the night of the accident I strongly believe was all God orchestrated, and to top everything off, I even got my case thrown out of court.

After this situation, my life and the lives of many others were changed and affected dramatically because only God knew the end from the beginning. I wouldn't have anything happen differently than the way it did. With a lot of prayer and faith I've learned so much. I started looking hard into the words of the Bible. At the rehab hospital was the first time I heard that my condition as a quadriplegic was supposed to be permanent. My reply to that was, "The devil is a liar."

I have read in the Bible that, with men, some things are impossible. But with God (Jesus is His name), all things are possible, including my healing and complete wholeness from this alleged quadriplegia. One day very soon, I am going to hop, skip, jump, and do a couple of cartwheels while I'm at it for His honor and His glory.

One thing that I've grown to realize is that eternity after this life is over is for a long time and a little bit more. I got these words from a minister I like to watch on TV from Texas. The way I heard it put is, imagine the tallest mountain in the world and you had a little bird that would never die and a small handkerchief that would never wear out. If once every thousand years, that little bird was to fly to the top of the mountain and pass over it with the handkerchief until the mountain was worn even with the ground, one second of eternity would not have even passed by. Now that's a long time.

Because I care about your eternity please read John 3:16, which says, "For God so loved the world that He gave His only begotten Son, that whoever believes in Him shall not perish but have everlasting life" (NKJV) now that's a lot of love. Check out how simple that is; it doesn't say that God loved the rich person or the person that took college courses. It doesn't say that God loved the white person or the black person or even the brown person. It says for God so loved the world, that includes anyone and everyone. All we have to do is believe in Him (the Son of God, Jesus) so we won't die (eternally) but have everlasting life. If that's what the Word says, and it does, then that's it. Hopefully this will help you understand the words that are coming. (Romans 10:10 NKJV) says, "For with the heart one believes unto righteousness, and with the mouth confession is made unto salvation." Read these two also: "That if you confess with your mouth the Lord Jesus and believe in your heart that God raised Him from the dead, you will be saved" (Romans 10:9 NKJV) and in verse 13, "For whoever calls on the name of the Lord shall be saved."

Another important passage reads, "And now abide faith, hope, love, these three; but the greatest of these is love" (1 Corinthians 13:13

NKJV). The word *love* in this verse, in the original Greek language is the word *agape*, which is the God kind of unconditional love (or Jesus if you want to get deep).

Check these two out: [8]"He who does not love does not know God, for God is love. [16]And we have known and believed the love that God has for us. God is love, and he who abides in love abides in God, and God in him" (1 John 4:8,16 NKJV). That's pretty heavy-duty. You would be wise to go over those previous few lines and let them marinate in your brain for a few minutes before going on.

Again in the book of John, we read, "In the beginning was the Word, and the Word was with God, and the Word was God" (John 1:1 KJV).

Follow me; just two more please. "And the Word was made flesh, and dwelt among us" (John 1:14 KJV). If you take the time to carefully read that verse, you can tell that it's talking about Jesus Christ. The last one is from 1 John. It reads, "Jesus Christ. This is the true God, and eternal life" (1 John 5:20 KJV). Now if that doesn't get you excited, your wood must be wet.

Oh, let me throw this one in for free. "Therefore, to him who knows to do good and does not do it, to him it is sin" (James 4:17 NKJV) and the Word says no one with sin will enter heaven and stay there. Now the ball is in your court; it's totally up to you. If you would like eternal life, ask Jesus to forgive you of all your sins. Tell Him you make Him your Lord and Savior; mean it from the heart; and, at the end, say, "In the name of Jesus, Amen" and you're in like Flynn.

If you just did that for the first time or if you're rededicating yourself, congratulations and welcome to the family of God. He gave me these words for myself, I believe they will help you out also, so remember them: Don't you let anybody, anything, or any word from anybody steal your peace in any way, shape, or form. God bless you, and I mean it when I say I (agape) love you like a young brother or a beautiful, young sister in the Lord. And I would like for you to have a super great and safe rest of the day or night (depending on the time) and even better morning, in Jesus's mighty name. Look for the next book. Thank you and May God bless you.

Milton Keynes UK
Ingram Content Group UK Ltd.
UKHW010320150624
443933UK00002BA/34

9 798890 316745